Knits, Knots, Buttons, and Bows

Knits, Knots, Buttons, and Bows

PROJECTS FOR BABIES

Lynda Schar

Martingale®
& COMPANY

Credits

President ■ Nancy J. Martin

CEO ■ Daniel J. Martin

COO ■ Tom Wierzbicki

Publisher ■ Jane Hamada

Editorial Director ■ Mary V. Green

Managing Editor ■ Tina Cook

Technical Editor ■ Ursula Reikes

Copy Editor ■ Durby Peterson

Design Director ■ Stan Green

Illustrator ■ Robin Strobel

Cover Designer ■ Stan Green

Text Designer ■ Regina Girard

Photographer ■ Brent Kane

Knits, Knots, Buttons, and Bows:
Projects for Babies
© 2006 by Lynda Schar

Martingale®
& C O M P A N Y

Martingale & Company
20205 144th Avenue NE
Woodinville, WA 98072-8478 USA
www.martingale-pub.com

Printed in China

11 10 09 08 07 06   8 7 6 5 4 3 2 1

Mission Statement

Dedicated to providing quality products and service to inspire creativity.

Library of Congress Cataloging-in-Publication Data

Library of Congress Control Number: 2006008463

ISBN-13: 978-1-56477-659-4
ISBN-10: 1-56477-659-X

Dedication

To my three daughters: Michelle, Sarah, and Vanessa

In memory of Hallie

For you created my inmost being;
You knit me together in my mother's womb.
Psalm 139:13 (New International Version)

Acknowledgments

First and foremost, I thank God for leading me through my life's journey.

Second, I thank my husband, Kurt, who has been there in good times and bad, just as he promised me.

My gratitude also goes to my lifelong best friends, Anita Sandoval, Linda Kuhlmann, and Keith Haley.

I also thank Jane Robbins, knitter extraordinaire and knitting pal, whose encouragement and expertise were instrumental in writing this book, and Joan Sommerville, the yarn goddess who helped find the awesome yarn for the projects.

I would like to express my gratitude to knitters Nita Porter, Su Fennern, Margie Bibby, and Sarah Duval, and to my "knitting posse," Jennifer Peterson, Tracy Weeks, Jane Kirby, Debby Bradish, Wendy Ferrin, and especially Tony McCammon for being so encouraging throughout this process.

My gratitude also goes to my "book advisory committee," Muriel Simmons, Bethany Maul, and Paula Swanson, in addition to my neighbor Yvonne Carstensen. I thank all of you for your encouragement!

I also want to thank my two chosen sons, Timothy Schar and Philip Schar, my godson, Chase Gourley, and my son-in-law, Greg Huber.

In addition, I would like to express my gratitude to Debbie's Clayground for creating buttons and pins exclusively for this book.

Most of all, my appreciation goes to my mother, Joann Connor Price, who encouraged me to knit at an early age to relieve boredom, which started my love for knitting.

Contents

Introduction

I love babies. In fact, I love babies so much I gave birth to three beautiful daughters, Michelle, Sarah, and Vanessa.

The excitement I felt when I discovered their impending arrival was unparalleled. A flurry of knitting, sewing, and embroidery ensued. When I brought my first daughter home, her room was the perfect combination of red, yellow, and blue, with Winnie the Pooh ruling supreme as the chosen icon.

Now, I'd like to help you prepare for the babies in your life. Between these pages are projects that will broaden your scope of babywear while introducing new concepts about knitted fashions, from color to design. You will find a variety of projects—from a functional diaper bag to a fancy dress to an adorable bunny rabbit and everything in between—to help you be ready when the very newest addition to the family is delivered into this world.

In this book you will find projects for beginning to intermediate knitters, as well as some new and some age-old techniques that I'm sure you will enjoy trying. I have taken great care to find yarn that is washable as well as beautiful and soft against your baby's skin. The colors are fresh and new, and they appear in some of my favorite combinations. It was fun to select these yarns from all the wonderful yarns available. While I was designing these projects, my hope was that these clothes and items would be handed down through generations to be enjoyed by many. Whether knit by mothers, grandmothers, aunties, or friends, all the projects in this book are sure to be treasured for years to come.

I am delighted that you have chosen this book to help you or someone else prepare for what will surely be one of the best times of your life.

Lynda Schar

Knitting Basics

elow are some of the basic techniques you'll need for the patterns in this book.

Casting On

Long-tail cast on. Measure out a length of yarn (approximately ½" to 1" for each stitch to be cast on), make a slipknot, and place it on the right-hand needle. Place your thumb and index finger between the yarn ends so that the working yarn is around your index finger and the tail end is around your thumb. Secure the ends with your other fingers and hold your palm facing upward. *Bring the needle up through the loop on the thumb, pivot the needle toward the loop on the index finger, and insert the needle into this loop from back to front. Go back down through the loop on the thumb, drop the loop off the thumb, and tighten the resulting stitch on the needle. Repeat from * for the desired number of stitches.

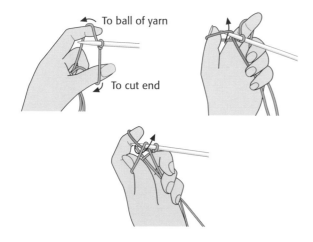

To ball of yarn

To cut end

Cable cast on. *Insert the right-hand needle between the first two stitches on the left-hand needle. Wrap the yarn around the right needle as if to knit and pull the yarn through to make a new stitch. Place the new stitch on the left needle. Repeat from * for the desired number of stitches.

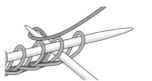

Insert the needle between 2 stitches. Knit a stitch.

Place the new stitch on the left needle.

Increases

Knit into front and back of the same stitch (K1f&b). Insert the right-hand needle knitwise into the stitch to be increased. Wrap the yarn around the needle and pull it through as if knitting, but leave the stitch on the left-hand needle. Insert the right-hand needle into the back of the same stitch, wrap the yarn around the needle, and pull it through. Slip the stitch from the left needle. You now have two stitches on the right-hand needle.

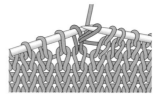

Knit into the stitch but do not drop it off the left needle.

Knit into the back of the same stitch.

Decreases

Knit two stitches together (K2tog). Insert the right-hand needle knitwise into the next two stitches on the left-hand needle and knit the two stitches as one.

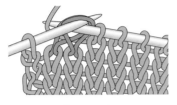

Knit 2 together.

Purl two stitches together (P2tog). Insert the right-hand needle purlwise into the next two stitches on the left-hand needle and purl the two stitches as one.

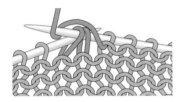

Purl 2 together.

Slip, slip, knit (ssk). Slip two stitches knitwise, one at a time, from the left-hand needle to the right-hand needle. Insert the left-hand needle into the front of these two slipped stitches and knit them together.

Slip 2 stitches to the right needle.   Knit 2 stitches together.

Binding Off

Knit the first stitch. *Knit the next stitch and pull the first stitch over the second stitch and off the needle. One stitch remains on the right-hand needle. Repeat from * until you have bound off the required number of stitches.

Pass the first knitted stitch over the second stitch.

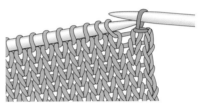

One bound-off knit stitch

I-Cord

Cast on the required number of stitches onto one double-pointed needle (if the stitches are already attached, skip this step). *Without turning the needle, slide the stitches to the other end of the needle, pull the yarn tightly around the back, and knit the stitches as usual. Repeat from * for desired length.

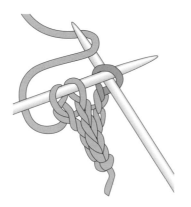

Seaming

Backstitch. Thread a needle with yarn. With wrong sides together, and working in the first row below the bind off, secure the beginning of the seam by bringing the yarn around the seam edges twice. Bring the needle back up approximately ¼" from where the yarn last emerged.

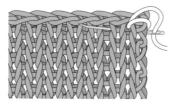

Insert the needle into the same place where the yarn emerged from the previous stitch, bring it back up approximately ¼" to the left, and pull the yarn through.

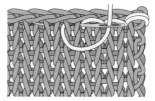

When seaming the vertical edges, work one stitch in from the edge. Repeat all around the sides of the pillow as directed, keeping the stitches even so that the edges don't pucker.

Kitchener (grafting) stitch. Place the stitches to be joined onto two separate needles. Hold the needles parallel, with the points facing to the right and with the right sides of the knitting facing outward. Thread a tapestry needle with the tail from the knitting or attach a new piece of yarn.

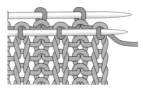

Place the stitches
on 2 needles.

1. Insert the tapestry needle through the first front stitch as if to purl and leave the stitch on the needle.

2. Insert the needle through the first back stitch as if to knit and leave the stitch on the needle.

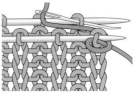

Steps 1 and 2

3. Insert the needle through the first front stitch as if to knit and slip this stitch off the needle. Insert the needle through the next front stitch as if to purl and leave the stitch on the needle.

4. Insert the needle through the first back stitch as if to purl. Slip that stitch off, bring the needle through the next back stitch as if to knit, and leave this stitch on the needle.

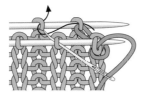

Steps 3 and 4

Repeat steps 3 and 4 until no stitches remain on the needle.

Invisible horizontal seam for shoulders. Line up the bound-off edges next to each other with right sides facing up. Thread a tapestry needle with yarn.

*Insert the needle under a stitch inside the bound-off edge of one side and under the corresponding stitch on the other side. Close the edge by pulling the yarn snugly enough to hide the bound-off edges, and repeat from * to the end. Note that you must have the same number of stitches on each piece to be joined.

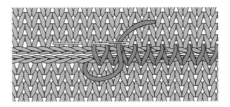

Invisible vertical seam for setting in sleeves. Thread a tapestry needle with yarn. Insert the needle under a stitch inside the bound-off edge of the vertical piece (bound-off sleeve). Insert the needle under either one or two horizontal bars between the first and second stitches of the horizontal piece (under one bar when the length of the vertical and horizontal piece is identical, and under two bars when easing in fullness). Continue taking stitches alternately from piece to piece. Pull the yarn gently after every five or six stitches.

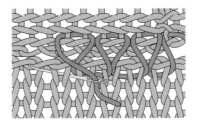

To ease in fullness, 2 horizontal bars are picked up along each bound-off edge.

Invisible vertical seam for side and underarm seams. Thread a tapestry needle with yarn. Insert the needle under the horizontal bar between the first and second stitches on one piece. Insert the needle into the corresponding bar on the other piece. Continue taking stitches alternately from side to side. Pull the yarn gently after every five or six stitches.

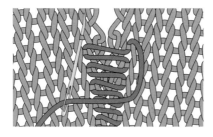

Slip-Stitch Crochet

Insert the crochet hook into the first stitch, yarn over hook, and pull through the stitch. *Insert the hook into the next stitch, yarn over hook, and pull through the stitch and the loop on the hook. Repeat from * around the edge. Make each loop a little loose so the edge won't be too tight.

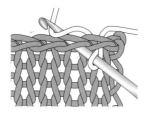
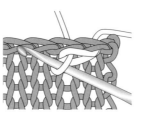

Blocking

I like to use the steam method. For this you will need a hand-held steamer or a steam iron. Never place the iron or steamer directly on the knitted piece. Place the pieces on a flat surface, hold steam above the pieces, and slowly work over the entire area. Let the steam dampen each piece completely. Sometimes it's a good idea to use a pressing cloth between the iron and the knitted pieces to protect the surface from intense heat and keep it clean. Shape the pieces as needed, pinning if desired, and let them dry completely. After sewing all the pieces together, I like to lightly steam the entire garment one more time for a finished look.

Abbreviations and Glossary

approx approximately

beg begin(ning)

BO bind off

CC contrasting color

CO cast on

cont continue

dec(s) decrease(ing)(s)

dpn(s) double-pointed needle(s)

EOR every other row

g gram(s)

garter st garter stitch [knit every row]

inc increase(ing)(s)

K knit

K1f&b knit into front and back of same stitch [1 stitch increase]

K2tog knit 2 stitches together [1 stitch decrease]

K3tog knit 3 stitches together [2 stitch decrease]

kw knitwise

m meter(s)

MB make bobble

MC main color

mm millimeter(s)

oz ounce(s)

P purl

P2tog purl 2 stitches together [1 stitch decrease]

P3tog purl 3 stitches together [2 stitch decrease]

patt pattern(s)

pm place marker

psso pass slipped stitch over

PU pick up and knit [with right side facing you unless instructed otherwise]

pw purlwise

rem remain(ing)

rep(s) repeat(s)

rnd(s) round(s)

RS right side

sl slip

sl 1 slip 1 stitch [slip stitch purlwise with yarn in back unless instructed otherwise]

ssk slip 2 stitches knitwise, 1 at a time, to right needle; then insert left needle from left to right into front loops and knit the 2 stitches together [1 stitch decrease]

st(s) stitch(es)

St st stockinette stitch [knit on right side rows, purl on wrong side rows]

tbl through back loop(s)

tog together

work even continue in pattern without increasing or decreasing

WS wrong side

wyib with yarn in back

wyif with yarn in front

yd(s) yard(s)

YO(s) yarn over(s)

Hush Little Baby: Blanket

This is a great take-along project that is completely reversible. The yarn knits up nicely, and if the blanket becomes your baby's favorite, it's washable.

Skill Level

■□□□ Beginner

Size

One size

Finished Measurements

36" x 36"

Materials

- 220 Superwash from Cascade Yarns (100% superwash wool; 100 g/3.5 oz; 220 yds) in the following amounts and colors: (4)

  MC 3 balls • color 833 Red

  CC1 1 ball • color 850 Green

  CC2 3 balls • color 831 Pink

- Size 8 needles or size required to obtain gauge

Gauge

18 sts and 24 rows = 4" in garter st

There is no finer investment for any community than putting milk into babies. Healthy citizens are the greatest asset any country can have.

—Winston Churchill

Triangles (Make 4)

Leave long tails of yarn for sewing seams.

- With MC, CO 162 sts and knit 2 rows. Then work as follows:

  Row 1: K1, ssk, knit to last 3 sts, K2tog, K1.

  Row 2: Knit.

  Rep rows 1 and 2 for total of 42 rows or 21 ridges. (2 rows of garter st = 1 ridge.)

- Change to CC1 and work rows 1 and 2 for 18 rows or 9 ridges.

- Change to CC2 and work rows 1 and 2 until 4 sts rem.

- On next RS row, ssk, K2tog. Knit 1 row and BO all sts.

Finishing

Starting at MC edge and referring to diagram below, and using the long tails of yarn to match each section of color, sew pieces 1 and 2 tog, then sew pieces 3 and 4 tog. Sew 2 halves together to make square. See box at right for seaming garter-st edges.

Seaming Garter-Stitch Edges

Look at the garter-stitch edge and you'll see a little knot at the edge of every row. You'll be working into the strand of this knot that wraps around the edge. With a yarn needle and yarn, and working back and forth between the pieces, insert the needle under the strand on one side, and then under the strand on the other side. Draw the yarn through loosely, stitch by stitch; then tighten it up after you've worked four or five stitches.

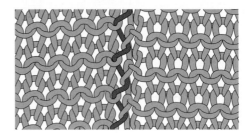

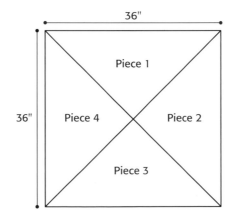

Baby, It's You! Dress and Hat

Every little girl needs a sweet little lacy number that her family and friends will ooh and aah over. This dress is fun to knit and will flatter your baby as she's twirled across the room or handed to each relative in turn.

Skill Level

◖■□□ Easy

Size

6 to 9 (12 to 18) months

Finished Measurements

Chest: 20 (21½)"

Length: 17 (19)"

Hat circumference: 17½"

Materials

- 5 (6) skeins of Pima Tencel from Cascade Yarns (50% Peruvian pima cotton, 50% tencel; 50 g/1.75 oz; 109 yds/135 m) in color 1317 Pink. Alternate garment shown on page 23 was made in color 7013 Teal. (4)
- Size 6 circular needle (16")
- Size 7 needles or size required to obtain gauge
- Size 7 circular needle (16") and double-pointed needles
- 1 snap or button, 1½" diameter

Gauge

20 sts and 26 rows = 4" in St st on larger needles

We haven't all had the good fortune to be ladies; we haven't all been generals, or poets, or statesmen; but when the toast works down to the babies, we stand on common ground.

—Mark Twain

Lace Pattern

Multiple of 11

Row 1 (RS): *Ssk, K3 tbl, YO, K1, YO, K3 tbl, K2tog, rep from * to end.

Rows 2, 4, 6: Purl.

Row 3: *Ssk, K2 tbl, YO, K1, YO, ssk, YO, K2 tbl, K2tog, rep from * to end.

Row 5: *Ssk, K1 tbl, YO, K1, (YO, ssk) twice, YO, K1 tbl, K2tog, rep from * to end.

Row 7: *Ssk, YO, K1, (YO, ssk) 3 times, YO, K2tog, rep from * to end.

Row 8: Purl.

Wide Ribbing Pattern

Multiple of 11

Row 1: *K1, P1, K7, P1, K1, rep from * to end.

Row 2: *P1, K1, P7, K1, P1, rep from * to end.

Rep rows 1 and 2 for patt.

Dress

Front

- With larger needles, CO 99 (110) sts. Work lace patt once. Beg wide ribbing patt and cont until piece measures 10½ (11½)", ending with WS row. For 12 to18 months only, on last row of ribbing dec 1 st at each side—99 (108) sts.

- **Dec row for 6 to 9 months:** K1, *K2tog, rep from * to end—50 sts.

- **Dec row for 12 to 18 months:** *K2tog, rep from * to end—54 sts.

- Work in St st until top measures 2 (2½)" from dec row, ending with WS row.

- **Armholes:** BO 5 sts at beg of next 2 rows. K2tog at each edge of next 3 RS rows—34 (38) sts. Work in St st until top measures 4½ (5)" from dec row, ending with WS row.

- **Beg neck shaping:** K10 (12), BO 14 sts, finish row.

- **Right neck:** Purl 1 row. K2tog at neck edge, knit to end. Purl 1 row. *K2tog at neck edge, knit to last st, K1f&b at armhole edge. Purl 1 row. Rep from * once—9 (11) sts. Work even for 7 rows. BO rem sts.

- **Left neck:** Join yarn at left neck edge on WS, P2tog, purl to end. Knit 1 row. *P2tog at neck edge, purl to end. K1f&b at armhole edge, knit to end. Rep from * once—9 (11) sts. Work even for 8 rows. BO rem sts.

Back

- Work as for front up to armhole decs—34 (38) sts. Cont until top measures 3½ (4)" from dec row, ending with WS row.

- **Beg neck shaping:** K15 (17), BO 4 sts, finish row.

- **Left neck:** Work until piece measures 1½ (2)" from beg of neck shaping, ending with WS row. BO 4 sts at neck edge, knit to end. Purl 1 row. (BO 1 st at neck edge, knit to end, purl 1 row) twice—9 (11) sts. Work even for 4 rows. BO rem sts.

- **Right neck:** Attach yarn at neck edge on WS, purl to end. Work in St st until piece measures 1½ (2)" from beg of neck shaping, ending with RS row. BO 4 sts at neck edge, purl to end. Knit 1 row. (BO 1 st at neck edge and purl to end, knit 1 row) twice—9 (11) sts. Work even for 4 rows. BO rem sts.

- **Plackets:** On left-hand side, starting at bottom of neck shaping, PU 10 sts to neck. Work in St st for 4 rows. BO all sts. On right-hand side, starting at top, PU 10 sts. Work 4 rows. (If you plan to use button, make buttonhole by K2tog, YO in middle of 2nd row. Attach plackets at bottom edge and finish placket by weaving bottom edge (beg with left side, right side will overlap left) to top of gap.

Sleeves

- With larger needles, CO 55 sts. Work lace patt once.

- Beg wide ribbing patt and cont in patt while working sleeve cap as follows: BO 5 sts at beg of

next 2 rows. K2tog at each end of next 2 RS rows. Work next row even. BO 2 sts at beg of next 6 rows. BO 3 sts at beg of next 4 rows. BO 5 sts at beg of next 2 rows. BO rem 7 sts.

Finishing

- Sew shoulder seams.

- **Neckband:** With smaller 16" circular needle, PU even number of sts starting at left placket and ending at right placket. Purl 1 row. Work in picot BO on RS as follows: BO 2 sts, *sl st back to left-hand needle, using cable CO method CO 3 sts, then BO 5 sts, rep from * to end. Fasten off.

- Sew sleeves into armholes. Sew side seams.

- Sew on button or snap.

- Weave in ends.

- Block dress.

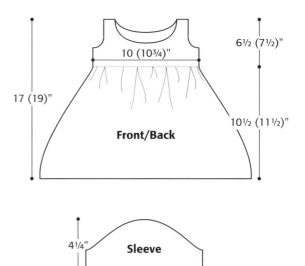

6½ (7½)"

10 (10¾)"

17 (19)"

10½ (11½)"

Front/Back

4¼" **Sleeve**

11"

Hat

Switch to dpns when necessary.

- With larger 16" circular needle, CO 88 sts. Join into rnd and pm. Work lace patt in the round 1 time, knitting purl rows. Knit every rnd until hat measures 4½" from beg.

- Work dec as follows:
  *K9, K2tog, rep from * to around—80 sts.
  Knit 1 rnd.

*K8, K2tog, rep from * to around—72 sts.
Knit 1 rnd.
*K7, K2tog, rep from * to around—64 sts.
Knit 1 rnd.
*K6, K2tog, rep from * to around—56 sts.
Knit 1 rnd.
*K5, K2tog, rep from * to around—48 sts.
*K4, K2tog, rep from * to around—40 sts.
*K3, K2tog, rep from * to around—32 sts.
*K2, K2tog, rep from * to around—24 sts.
*K1, K2tog, rep from * to around—16 sts.
K2tog around until 2 sts rem on needle.

- Work I-cord (see page 12) on rem 2 sts for 1½".
  BO 2 sts, pull tail of cord through to WS, and
  weave in end.

- Block hat.

4½"

Hat

17½"

Baby Boomer: Vest

It's never too early to dress your little boy in preppy clothes. Combine this vest with a nice pair of khakis, a white shirt, and oxford shoes, and your baby will be ready to learn the rules of fashion.

Skill Level

◖■□□ Easy

Size

3 to 6 (9 to 12, 18) months

Finished Measurements

Chest size: 19 (20½, 22)"

Length: 9½ (10½, 11½)"

> *Babies do not want to hear about babies; they like to be told of giants and castles.*
>
> —Dr. Samuel Johnson

Materials

- Pima Silk from Frog Tree (85% pima cotton, 15% silk; 50 g; 155 yds) in the following amounts and colors: **4**

  MC 1 skein • color 850 Purple

  CC 1 skein • color 841 Blue

- Size 6 needles
- Size 7 needles or size required to obtain gauge

Gauge

20 sts and 28 rows = 4" in St st on larger needles

Ribbing Pattern

Multiple of 4

Row 1: *K3, P1, rep from * to end.

Row 2: *K2, P1, K1, rep from * to end.

Rep rows 1 and 2 for patt.

Back

When changing colors, carry yarns loosely up side.

- With small needles and MC, CO 48 (52, 56) sts. Work 6 rows in ribbing patt.

- Change to large needles and CC. Work in St st alternating 6 rows of CC and 6 rows of MC until piece measures 5 (5½, 6)" from CO edge, ending with WS row.

- **Armholes:** Cont in stripe patt, BO 2 sts at beg of next 4 rows, then dec 1 st at each side of next 3 rows—34 (38, 42) sts.

- Cont working in St st until piece measures 4 (4½, 5)" from beg of armhole, ending with WS row.

- **Next row (RS):** K12 (13, 15), BO 10 (12, 12) sts, finish row.

- **Left neck and shoulder:** Purl 1 row. BO 2 sts at neck edge, knit to end—10 (11, 13) sts. Purl 1 row. BO rem sts.

- **Right neck and shoulder:** With WS facing you, attach yarn at neck edge and BO 2 sts, purl to end—10 (11, 13) sts. Knit 1 row. Purl 1 row. BO rem sts.

Front

- Work same as back until armhole decs are complete. Cont in St st until piece measures 1½ (1¾, 2)" from beg of armhole.

- **V-neck shaping:** K16 (18, 20), attach 2nd ball of yarn and BO 2 sts, finish row. Working both sides AT SAME TIME, on RS rows only, dec 1 st at neck edge 3 times, then every 4 rows 3 (4, 4) times—10 (11, 13). Work even until front measures same as back. BO rem sts.

Finishing

- Sew right shoulder seam tog.

- **Neckband:** With smaller needles and MC, starting at top of left front, PU 20 (21, 23) sts along left front neck, 2 sts at center, 20 (21, 23) sts along right front neck, and 14 (16, 16) sts across back—56 (60, 64) sts. Beg with row 2 of ribbing patt and work 4 rows. BO kw with WS facing you.

- Sew left neck and shoulder seam.

- **Armhole bands:** With smaller needles and MC, PU 60 (64, 68) sts along armhole edge. Work ribbing as for neck.

- Sew side seams.

- Weave in ends.

- Block vest.

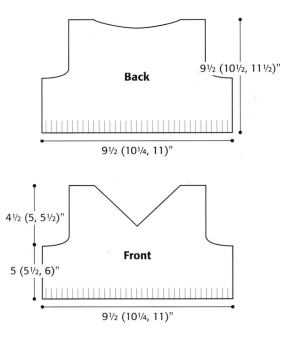

Back
9½ (10½, 11½)"
9½ (10¼, 11)"

Front
4½ (5, 5½)"
5 (5½, 6)"
9½ (10¼, 11)"

Be My Baby: Chanel-Style Suit and Bag

Your baby girl will wow them in the streets with her haute couture suit plus bag made by someone who loves her. Worn with white stockings and patent leather shoes, this outfit will make her ready for any occasion.

Skill Level

■■□□ Easy

Size

12 (18, 24) months

Finished Measurements

Jacket chest: 19½ (20½, 22½)"
Jacket length: 11½ (12¼, 13)"
Skirt length: 7½ (7¾, 8)"
Bag: 7" wide x 4½" high (excluding handle)

Materials

- **MC** 3 hanks of Ultramerino 6 from Artyarns (100% merino wool; 274 yds) in color 126 **4**
- **CC** 1 hank of Wool Fur from Artyarns (95% wool, 5% nylon; 84 yds) in color 126 **6**
- Size 7 needles or size required to obtain gauge
- Size 11 needles
- Size 11 circular needle (16") for bag
- ¾"-wide elastic, enough to go around waist plus 2"

Gauge

22 sts and 28 rows = 4" in St st with MC on smaller needles

I just can't get over how much babies cry. I really had no idea what I was getting into. To tell you the truth, I thought it would be more like getting a cat.

—Anne Lamott

Skirt

- With larger needles and CC, CO 110 sts for all sizes; join into rnd and pm. With smaller needles and MC, K1f&b of each st—220 sts.

- Knit in the round for 7½ (7¾, 8)" from beg. Purl next row to create fold line for casing.

- Knit until skirt measures 9 (9¼, 9½)" from beg. BO all sts.

- Fold top casing at fold line and stitch to skirt. Leave opening to put elastic through.

- Cut piece of elastic to fit your baby's waist plus 2". Average is about 22" for 12-month-old. Thread elastic through casing, sew ends tog, and close opening.

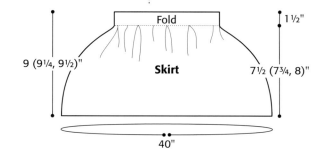

Jacket

Back

- With larger needles and CC, CO 26 (28, 30) sts. Switch to smaller needles and MC, K1f&b of each st—52 (56, 60) sts.

- Purl 2 rows. Work in St st until back measures 6½ (7, 7½)" from beg, ending with WS row.

- **Armholes:** BO 3 sts at beg of next 2 rows. BO 2 sts at beg of next 2 rows. BO 1 st at beg of next 2 rows—40 (44, 48) sts. Work until back measures 4 (4¼, 4½)" from beg of armhole, ending with WS row.

- **Beg shoulder and neck shaping:** BO 3 sts at beg of next 2 rows—34 (38, 42) sts. On next row, BO 3 sts, K11 (13, 15), BO 6 sts, finish row.

- **Left shoulder and neck:** With WS facing you, BO 3 sts at side, purl to end. BO 2 sts at neck, knit to end. Purl 1 row. K2tog at neck, knit to end. BO 5 sts at side, purl to end. K2tog at neck, knit to end. BO rem 2 (4, 6) sts.

- **Right shoulder and neck:** Attach yarn to neck edge with WS facing you. BO 2 sts at neck, purl to end. Knit 1 row. P2tog at neck, purl to end. BO 5 sts at side, knit to end. P2tog at neck, purl to end. BO rem 2 (4, 6) sts.

Left Front

- With larger needles and CC, CO 14 (15, 16) sts. Switch to smaller needles and MC, K1f&b of each st—28 (30, 32) sts.

- Purl 2 rows. Work in St st until front measures 6½ (7, 7½)" from beg, ending with WS row.

- **Armhole:** BO 3 sts at side, knit to end. Purl 1 row. BO 2 sts at side, knit to end. Purl 1 row. BO 1 st at side, knit to end—22 (24, 26) sts. Work until piece measures 3 (3¼, 3½)" from beg of armhole, ending with RS row.

- **Neck and shoulder shaping:** BO 2 sts at neck, purl to end. *Knit to last 2 sts, K2tog at neck. P2tog at neck, purl to end. Rep from * 2 more times. With RS facing you, BO 3 sts at side, knit to end. P2tog at neck, purl to end. BO 3 sts at side, knit to end. Purl 1 row. BO 5 sts at side, knit to end. Purl 1 row. BO rem 2 (4, 6) sts.

Right Front

- Work as for left front to armholes, ending with RS row.

- **Armhole:** BO 3 sts at side, purl to end. Knit 1 row. BO 2 sts at side, purl to end. Knit 1 row. BO 5 sts at side, purl to end—22 (24, 26) sts. Work until piece measures 3 (3¼, 3½)" from beg of armhole, ending with WS row.

- **Neck and shoulder shaping:** BO 2 sts at neck, knit to end. *Purl to last 2 sts, P2tog at neck. K2tog at neck, knit to end. Rep from * 2 more times. With WS facing you, BO 3 sts at side, purl to end. K2tog at neck, knit to end. BO 3 sts at side, purl to end. Knit 1 row. BO 5 sts at side, purl to end. Knit 1 row. BO rem 2 (4, 6) sts.

Sleeves

- With larger needles and CC, CO 14 (16, 18) sts; turn work. Switch to smaller needles and MC, K1f&b of each st—28 (32, 36) sts.

- Purl 2 rows. Work in St st, inc 1 st at each side every 8 rows 5 times—38 (42, 46) sts. Work even until piece measures 6½ (6¾, 7)".

- **Shape cap:** BO 4 sts at beg of next 4 rows. BO 4 (4, 5) sts at beg of next 5 rows—2 (6, 5) sts. BO rem sts.

Finishing

- Sew shoulder seams.

- Sew sleeves in. Sew side seams.

- Weave in all ends.

- **Front trim:** With smaller needles, RS facing you, and MC, PU even number of sts along each front edge (beg at bottom edge for right front and beg at top edge for left front). Turn and purl to end. Switch to larger needles and CC, BO as follows: K2tog, *K2tog, lift back stitch over front stitch to BO, rep from * to end.

- **Collar:** With smaller needles, RS facing you, and MC, PU 10 (12, 12) sts from neck to shoulder seam, 14 sts across back and 10 (12, 12) sts from shoulder to neck—34 (38, 38) sts. Purl 1 row. Knit 2 rows. Purl 1 row. BO all sts. Fold collar toward inside and sew in place.

- Block gently.

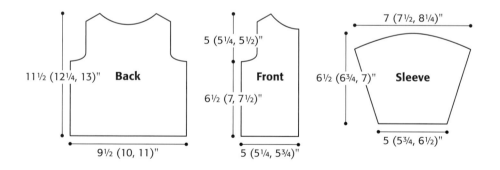

11½ (12¼, 13)" **Back**

9½ (10, 11)"

5 (5¼, 5½)"

Front

6½ (7, 7½)"

5 (5¼, 5¾)"

7 (7½, 8¼)"

6½ (6¾, 7)" **Sleeve**

5 (5¾, 6½)"

Bag

- With circular needle and CC, CO 34 sts, pm after 17 sts and at beg of rnd. (Your yarn will stretch around.) Join into rnd.

    Rnd 1: At beg of rnd, K1f&b, knit to marker and sl marker, K1f&b in next st—36 sts.

    Rnd 2: Knit.

    Work rnds 1 and 2 another 2 times—40 sts.

- **Next 3 rnds:** K2tog after each marker for 3 rnds. BO all sts—34 sts.

- With WS tog, sew bottom tog using whipstitch.

- **Strap:** With dpn, CO 3 sts and make piece of I-cord 15" long (see page 12). BO all sts. Sew one end of strap to each side of bag.

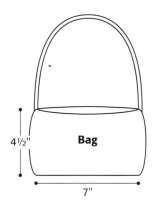

Bag

4½"

7"

Baby Love: Vest

Nothing says stylish and chic like a cute little pullover vest. Every baby will want one.

Skill Level

■□□□ Beginner

Size

One size

Finished Measurements

Chest: 23"
Length: 10¼"

Materials

- 2 skeins of Romance from Kollage Yarns (50% silk, 33% bamboo, 15% polyamide, 2% rayon; 68 g; 100 yds) in color Pink Cloud ④
- Size 10½ needles or size required to obtain gauge

Gauge

18 sts and 20 rows = 4" in garter st

When I got home from the hospital, I felt lucky when Daniel went more than two hours without nursing. To survive, I just cradled him next to me and we slept. On the bed, on a couch, in a chair. It didn't matter where. I could have slept on an ice-cold concrete floor. Like a baby.

That was the first month.

The second month, we woke up.

—Betty Holcomb

Front/Back

- CO 52 sts. Work in garter st until piece measures 5½" from beg.

- **Armholes:** BO 3 sts at beg of next 2 rows. K2tog at beg of next 3 rows—40 sts. Work even until piece measures 2½" from beg of armholes, ending with WS row.

- **Beg neck shaping:** K16, BO 8 sts, finish row.

- **Right neck:** Knit to neck edge. BO 2 sts at neck, knit to end. *Knit 1 row. BO 1 st at neck, knit to end. Rep from * 3 more times—10 sts. Knit 1 row. BO rem sts.

- **Left neck:** Attach yarn at neck edge and BO 2 sts, knit to end. *Knit 1 row. BO 1 st at neck, knit to end. Rep from * 3 more times—10 sts. Knit 2 rows. BO rem sts.

Finishing

- Sew shoulder seams.
- Sew side seams.
- Weave in ends.
- Block vest.

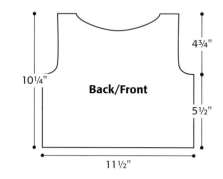

10¼" 4¾" **Back/Front** 5½" 11½"

Sweet, Sweet, Baby: Poncho and Hat

All baby girls need to learn to accessorize. Not only is this poncho and hat set the latest thing, it's soft and warm and will pump up any outfit into high style.

Skill Level

■■□□ Easy

Size

One size

Finished Measurements

Poncho length: 12"

Hat circumference: 17"

Materials

- 2 skeins of Passion from Kollage Yarns (42% polyamide, 35% rayon, 14% nylon, 9% metallic polyester; 90 g; 100 yds) in color Black Cherry 🔟
- Size 13 needles and double-pointed needles or size required to obtain gauge
- **Optional:** 1 button or pin for decoration

Gauge

10 sts and 12 rows = 4" in garter st

I hardly had a new baby for two weeks when it hit me that I was never again going to be rested. Well, maybe not never. I had some wisp of hope that perhaps when the kid went off to college, I'd get a full night's sleep again. I could sure as hell see it wasn't going to be during his infancy.

—Sandi Kahn Shelton

Poncho

Front

- CO 2 sts. K1f&b in both sts—4 sts.
- **Inc rows:** (K1f&b, knit to last st, K1f&b) on every row until there are 54 sts on needle and work measures 7" from bottom point.
- **Dec rows:** (K1, K2tog to last 3 sts, ssk, K1) on every row until there are 20 sts on needle and work measures 12" from bottom point, ending on WS row.
- **Beg neck shaping:** K1, K2tog, K5, BO 4, K5, ssk, K1.
- **Right neck:**

  Row 1: K1, K2tog, K4—6 sts.

  Row 2: BO 2 sts at neck, ssk, K1—3 sts.

  Row 3: Knit.

  Row 4: BO rem sts.

- **Left neck:** With WS facing you, join yarn at neck edge.

  Row 1: BO 2 sts at neck, K1, ssk, K1—4 sts.

  Row 2: K1, K2tog, K1—3 sts.

  Row 3: Knit.

  Row 4: BO rem sts.

Poncho Back

Work as for front, reversing shaping.

Poncho Finishing

- Sew seam along left-hand side. Sew seam along right-hand side, leaving 2" free at neck to make it easy to pull poncho over child's head.
- Weave in ends.
- Pin neck edges tog with decorative pin, or securely sew button on back piece at neck edge. There is no need to make buttonhole because fabric is loose enough for button to fit through.

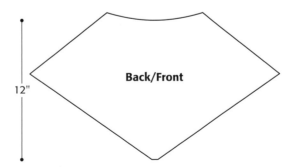

12"

Back/Front

Hat

- Using dpns, CO 42 sts onto 3 needles (14 on each). Knit around until hat measures 3½" from beg.
- Dec as follows:

  *K5, K2tog, rep from * around—36 sts.

  Knit 1 rnd.

  *K4, K2tog, rep from * around—30 sts.

  Knit 1 rnd.

  *K3, K2tog, rep from * around—24 sts.

  *K2, K2tog, rep from * around—18 sts.

  *K1, K2tog, rep from * around—12 sts.

  K2tog until 3 sts rem. Pull yarn through rem sts and fasten off.
- Weave in end.

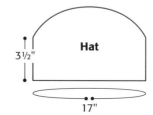

3½" **Hat**

17"

Angel Baby: A-Line Dress and Bloomers

Whether Baby is playing on the beach, going to a tea party, or accompanying Mom to the mall, this combo is the perfect outfit and is sure to catch everyone's eye.

Skill Level

■■□□ Easy

Size

12 (18, 24) months

Finished Measurements

Chest: 20½ (22, 24)"
Dress length: 14 (15, 15½)"
Bloomers length: 13½ (14¼, 15)"

Materials

- Sierra from Cascade Yarns (80% pima cotton, 20% wool; 100 g/3.5 oz; 191 yds) in the following amounts and colors: (4)

  Dress 2 (2, 3) skeins • color 86 Variegated Pink

  Bloomers 2 (2, 3) skeins • color 17 Pink

- Size 6 needles
- Size 7 needles or size required to obtain gauge
- Size 7 (4.5 mm) crochet hook
- 2 buttons, 1" diameter
- ½"-wide elastic, enough for waist measurement plus 2"
- ¼"-wide elastic, enough to go around both legs plus 2"
- Safety pin
- Twill tape to match yarn

Gauge

20 sts and 26 rows = 4" in St st on larger needles

> *People who say they sleep like a baby usually don't have one.*
>
> —Leo J. Burke

Scallop Edge

Multiple of 6 + 5

Row 1 (RS): *(K1, P1) twice, K1, sl 1, rep from * to last 5 sts, (K1, P1) twice, K1.

Row 2: *(P1, K1) twice, P1, sl 1, rep from * to last 5 sts, (P1, K1) twice, P1.

A-Line Dress

Front

- With larger needles, CO 83 (89, 95) sts. Work scallop edge once. Work 2 rows in St st.

- **Dec:** (K1, K2tog, knit to last 3 sts, ssk, K1) every 4 rows 16 (17, 18) times—51 (55, 59) sts.

- **Armholes:** BO 4 sts at beg of next 2 rows. Dec 1 st at each side on next 2 RS rows—39 (43, 47) sts. Work in St st until piece measures 2" from beg of armhole, ending with WS row.

- **Beg neck shaping:** K13 (14, 15), BO 13 (15, 17) sts, finish row.

- **Right neck:** *Purl 1 row. K2tog at neck, knit to end. Rep from * once—11 (12, 13) sts. Work 11 rows in St st. BO all sts.

- **Left neck:** With WS facing you, attach yarn at neck, *P2tog and purl to end. Knit 1 row. Rep from * once—11 (12, 13) sts. Work 11 rows in St st. BO all sts.

Back

- Work same as for front including armholes.

- Work in St st until piece measures 3" from beg of armhole, ending with WS row.

- **Beg neck shaping:** K13 (14, 15), BO 13 (15, 17) sts, finish row.

- **Left neck:** *Purl 1 row. K2tog at neck, knit to end. Rep from * 1 time. Work 11 rows in St st. Buttonhole row: With RS facing you, K3 (4, 5), work buttonhole (see page 45), finish row. Purl 1 row. Dec row: K2tog, K7 (8, 9), K2tog. Purl 1 row. Dec row: K2tog, K5, K2tog—7 (8, 9) sts. Purl 1 row. BO all sts.

- **Right neck:** With WS facing you, attach yarn at neck, *P2tog at neck, purl to end. Knit 1 row. Rep from * 1 time. Work 11 rows in St st. Buttonhole row: With RS facing you, K3 (4, 5), work buttonhole, finish row. Purl 1 row. Dec row: K2tog, K7 (8, 9), K2tog. Purl 1 row. Dec row: K2tog, K5, K2tog—7 (8, 9) sts. Purl 1 row. BO all sts.

Finishing

- Sew side seams.

- With crochet hook, and starting at underarm, work 1 row of slip st crochet around armhole edges (see page 14).

- Sew buttons at each shoulder on front to correspond with buttonholes on back.

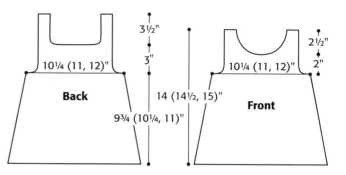

Bloomers

Side A

- With smaller needles, CO 113 sts (for all sizes). Work scallop edge once. Work 2 rows in St st. On next row, inc 1 st at each side—115 sts. Then inc 1 st at each side every 6 rows 2 times—119 sts. Work should measure approx 3".

- Cont in St st, BO sts at beg of rows as indicated, and finish row.

  Row 1 (RS): BO 3 sts.

  Row 2: BO 3 sts.

  Row 3: BO 2 sts.

  Row 4: BO 4 sts.

  Row 5: BO 2 sts.

  Row 6: BO 4 sts.

  Row 7: BO 2 sts.

Row 8: BO 4 sts.

Row 9: BO 2 sts.

Row 10: BO 2 sts.

K2tog at each side on next 4 RS rows—83 sts.

- Work in St st until piece measures 13½ (14½, 15)" from beg, ending with RS row.

- Knit next 2 rows to create fold line for casing.

- Work 5 rows in St st. BO all sts.

Side B

- Work same as Side A until dec rows.

- **Dec rows:** Cont in St st, BO sts at beg of rows as indicated and finish row.

  Row 1 (RS): BO 3 sts.

  Row 2: BO 3 sts.

Row 3: BO 4 sts.

Row 4: BO 2 sts.

Row 5: BO 4 sts.

Row 6: BO 2 sts.

Row 7: BO 4 sts.

Row 8: BO 2 sts.

Row 9: BO 2 sts.

Row 10: BO 2 sts.

K2tog at each side on next 4 RS rows—83 sts.

- Work in St st until piece measures 13½ (14½, 15)" from beg, ending with RS row.
- Knit next 2 rows to create fold line for casing.
- Work 5 rows in St st. BO all sts.

Finishing

- With WS of pieces A and B tog, sew tog along back seam and then front seam. Sew crotch tog.
- Fold top casing at fold line and sew, leaving about 2" open. Thread ½"-wide elastic through using safety pin. Overlap ends and sew them tog. Close opening.
- Sew twill tape to bottom of legs, about 2" from bottom. Leave open at seam. Cut ¼"-wide elastic and thread through using safety pin. Overlap ends and sew them tog. Sew twill tape down at seams.

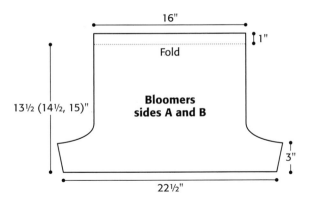

16"

1"

Fold

Bloomers sides A and B

13½ (14½, 15)"

3"

22½"

1-Row Buttonhole

Work to buttonhole, sl st pw wyif, *sl next st wyib from left needle, psso and rep from * 3 times more (don't move yarn). Sl last bound-off st to left needle and turn work.

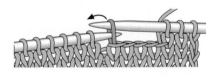

Using cable CO method, CO 5 sts.

Sl first st wyib from left needle and pass extra CO st over it to close buttonhole. Work to end of row.

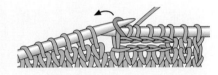

It's a Baby! Jeans and T-shirt

Inspired by Mr. Green Jeans on the "Captain Kangaroo" show, the green jeans with matching t-shirt will be everyone's favorite outfit when your baby sports this cute combo.

Skill Level

■■□□ Easy

Size

3 (6, 9, 12, 18) months

Finished Measurements

Chest: 18½ (20, 22, 23, 24½)"

T-shirt length: 11 (11¾, 12½, 13¼, 14)"

Pants length: 14½ (16¼, 17¾, 19½, 21)"

Materials

- Sierra from Cascade Yarns (80% pima cotton, 20% wool; 100 g/3.5 oz; 191 yds) in the following amounts and colors: (4)

  Jeans: 2 (2, 3, 3, 3) skeins • color 8 Green

  T-shirt: 2 skeins • color 81 Variegated Green
- Size 6 needles
- Size 7 needles or size required to obtain gauge
- ½"-wide elastic, enough to go around waist plus 2"
- Snap tape (optional)
- 1 button, ¾" diameter, for shirt

Gauge

20 sts and 26 rows = 4" in St st on larger needles

Families with babies and families without babies are sorry for each other.

—E. W. Howe

Jeans

One Half (Make 2)

- With smaller needles, CO 53 (53, 59, 59, 59) sts. Work in St st for 5 rows. Knit 1 row on WS to create fold line for hem. Switch to larger needles.

- Work 2 rows in St st.

- **Inc rows:** (K1f&b, knit to last 2 sts, K1f&b, K1) every 6 rows 9 (10, 11, 12, 13) times—71 (73, 81, 83, 85) sts. Work even until piece measures 8 (9½, 11, 12½, 14)" from beg, ending with WS row.

- **Dec rows:** BO 3 sts at beg of next 2 rows. BO 2 sts at beg of next 2 rows. Dec 1 st at each side on next 4 RS rows—53 (55, 63, 65, 67) sts.

- Cont in St st until piece measures 15½ (17¼, 18¾, 20½, 22)" from beg, ending with RS row.

- Knit 1 row on WS to create fold line for casing.

- Work 6 rows in St st. BO all sts.

Finishing

- Sew front and back seams.

- Sew inseams. (Optional: use snap tape on inseam.)

- Fold bottom hem at fold line and sew in place.

- Fold top casing at fold line and sew, leaving opening to insert elastic. Insert elastic, overlap ends, and sew together. Sew opening closed.

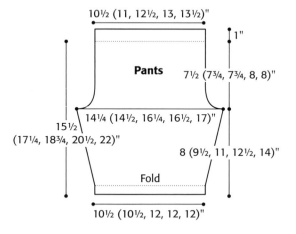

10½ (11, 12½, 13, 13½)"

1"

Pants

7½ (7¾, 7¾, 8, 8)"

14¼ (14½, 16¼, 16½, 17)"

15½ (17¼, 18¾, 20½, 22)"

8 (9½, 11, 12½, 14)"

Fold

10½ (10½, 12, 12, 12)"

T-shirt

Back

- With smaller needles, CO 46 (50, 54, 58, 62) sts. Work in St st for 5 rows. Knit 1 row on WS to create fold line for hem. Switch to larger needles and cont in St st until back measures 6¾ (7½, 8¼, 9, 9¾)" from beg, ending with WS row.

- **Armholes:** BO 2 (2, 2, 3, 3) sts at beg of next 2 rows. Dec 1 st at each side of next 4 (4, 5, 5, 6) RS rows as follows: K1, K2tog to last 3 sts, ssk, K1—34 (38, 40, 42, 44) sts. Cont in St st until back measures 10 (10¾, 11½, 12¼, 13)" from beg, ending with WS row.

- **Beg neck shaping:** K13 (14, 15, 15, 16), BO 8 (10, 10, 12, 12) sts, finish row.

- **Left neck:** Purl 1 row. BO 3 sts at neck, knit to end. Purl 1 row. BO 1 st at neck on EOR 2 times—8 (9, 10, 10, 11) sts. BO all sts.

- **Right neck:** With WS facing you, attach yarn at neck edge, BO 3 sts at neck, purl to end. Knit 1 row. BO 1 st at neck on EOR 2 times—8 (9, 10, 10, 11) sts. Work until back measures 11¾ (12½, 13¼, 14, 14¾)" from beg to top of shoulder. BO all sts.

Front

- Work as for back, including armhole shaping. Cont in St st until front measures 8¾ (9½, 10¼, 11, 11¾)" from beg, ending with WS row.

- **Beg neck shaping:** K14 (16, 17, 17, 18), BO 6 (6, 6, 8, 6) sts, finish row.

- **Right neck:** Purl 1 row. BO 2 (3, 3, 3, 3) sts at neck, knit to end. Purl 1 row. *BO 1 st at neck, knit to end. Purl 1 row. Rep from * 4 times—8 (9, 10, 10, 11) sts. Next RS row (buttonhole row): K2 (2, 3, 3, 3), make 4-st buttonhole (see page 45), finish row. Purl 1 row. Work 2 rows in St st. BO all sts.

- **Left neck:** With WS facing you, attach yarn at neck edge, BO 2 (3, 3, 3, 3) sts, purl to end. Knit 1 row. *BO 1 st at neck, purl to end. Knit 1 row. Rep from * 4 times—8 (9, 10, 10, 11) sts. Purl 1 row. Omit buttonhole row and work 4 rows in St st. BO all sts.

Sleeves (Make 2)

- With smaller needles, CO 22 (24, 26, 28, 30) sts. Work in St st for 5 rows. Knit 1 row on WS to create fold line for hem. Knit 1 row and inc 1 st at each side—24 (26, 28, 30, 32) sts. Switch to larger needles and working in St st, inc 1 st at each side every 6 rows 6 (7, 8, 9, 10) times—36 (38, 44, 48, 52) sts. Sleeve should measure approx 7¾ (8½, 9¼, 10, 10¾)". If not, work even until it does.

- **Cap shaping:** BO 3 (3, 4, 4, 4) sts at beg of next 2 rows. BO 2 sts at beg of next 8 rows. BO 3 sts at beg of next 2 rows. BO rem sts.

Finishing

- Sew short back strap to front strap buttonhole, starting at outside.
- **Neckband:** With RS facing you, and starting at left shoulder seam, PU 12 (13, 13, 14, 14) sts across back neck, and 20 (20, 20, 22, 22) sts across front—32 (33, 33, 36, 36) sts. Purl 1 row. BO all sts.
- Sew on button, and baste front to back at shoulder on button side so that you can insert sleeve.
- Sew sleeves. Sew side seams.
- Turn up bottom hem at fold line and sew in place.

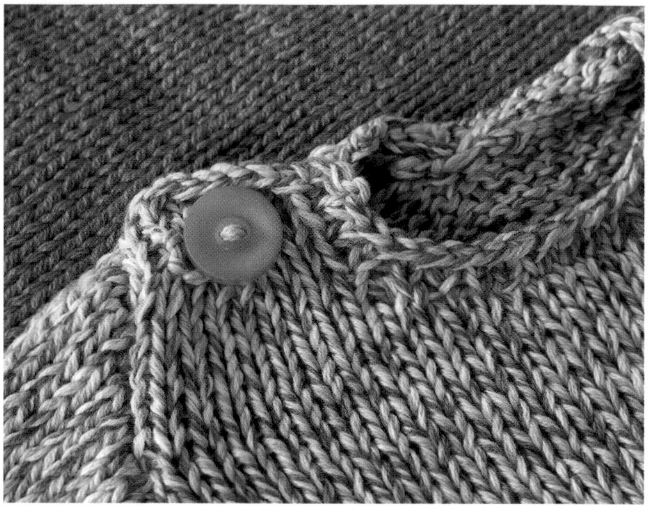

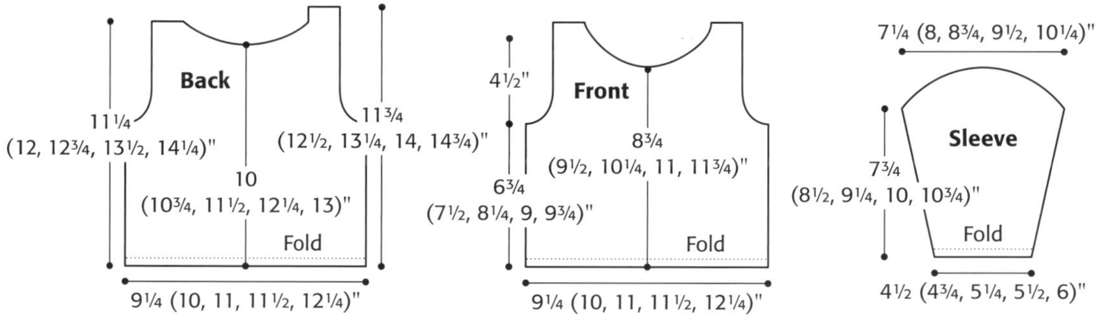

Back
11¼ (12, 12¾, 13½, 14¼)"
11¾ (12½, 13¼, 14, 14¾)"
10 (10¾, 11½, 12¼, 13)"
Fold
9¼ (10, 11, 11½, 12¼)"
Front
4½"
8¾ (9½, 10¼, 11, 11¾)"
6¾ (7½, 8¼, 9, 9¾)"
Fold
9¼ (10, 11, 11½, 12¼)"
7¼ (8, 8¾, 9½, 10¼)"
Sleeve
7¾ (8½, 9¼, 10, 10¾)"
Fold
4½ (4¾, 5¼, 5½, 6)"

Baby Talk: Pillows

When my babies were tiny it was always nice to have something to rest my arm on while holding them. These pillows squish to a small size and will travel anywhere you go.

Skill Level

◖■☐☐ Easy

Approximate Finished Measurements

Pillow A: 11" x 13"

Pillow B: 12" x 14"

Pillow C: 11½" x 13"

Materials

- 220 Superwash from Cascade Yarns (100% superwash wool; 100 g/3.5 oz; 220 yds) in the following amounts and colors: ④

Pillow A

MC 1 skein • color 842 Light Purple

CC 1 skein • color 843 Medium Purple

Pillow B

MC 1 skein • color 834 Pink

CC 1 skein • color 835 Salmon

Pillow C

1 skein • color 844 Blue

- Size 8 needles or size required to obtain gauge
- Batting or pillow form* for stuffing

Purchase pillow form after pillow is complete to ensure good fit.

Gauge

18 sts and 24 rows = 4"

Visitor—*"Well, Joe, how do you like your new little sister?"*

Joe—*"Oh, she's all right, I guess; but there are lots of things we needed worse."*

10,000 Jokes, Toasts & Stories

Pillow A

Herringbone Pattern

Multiple of 10 sts

Row 1 (RS): *K9, P1, rep from *.

Row 2: *P1, K1, P8, rep from *.

Row 3: *K7, P1, K1, P1, rep from *.

Row 4: *(P1, K1) 4 times, P2, rep from *.

Row 5: *K3, (P1, K1) 3 times, P1, rep from *.

Row 6: *(P1, K1) 3 times, P3, K1, rep from *.

Row 7: *K1, P1, K3, (P1, K1) twice, P1, rep from *.

Row 8: *(P1, K1) twice, P3, K1, P1, K1, rep from *.

Row 9: *(K1, P1) twice, K3, P1, K1, P1, rep from *.

Row 10: *(P1, K1) twice, P6, rep from *.

Row 11: *K7, P1, K2, rep from *.

Row 12: *P3, K1, P6, rep from *.

Rep rows 1–12 for patt.

Pillow

- **Front:** With MC, CO 60 sts. Work herringbone patt 6 times (total 72 rows). BO all sts. If you like, pm every 10 sts to keep track of each patt rep.

- **Back:** With CC, CO 60 sts and work in St st until back measures same as front.

- **Finishing:** Place WS of both pieces tog. With CC, PU 60 sts at top through both pieces. Work in seed st as follows, alternating 2 rows with CC and 2 with MC. Row 1: *K1, P1, rep from * to end.

Row 2: * P1, K1, rep from * to end. BO all sts. Rep for opposite (bottom) edge. Weave in ends. Sew rem sides with a backstitch (see page 12), leaving about 3" opening if stuffing pillow or 8" opening if using pillow form. Fold batting to size of pillow and insert into pillow, or insert pillow form. Sew opening closed.

Herringbone pattern

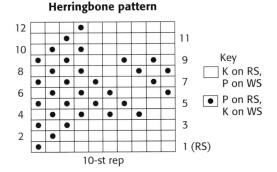

Key

☐ K on RS, P on WS

▣ P on RS, K on WS

10-st rep

Pillow B

Pillow

- **Front:** With MC, CO 63 sts and work patt 8 times, then work rows 1 and 2 one more time (total 82 rows). BO all sts.

- **Back:** With CC, work same as front.

- **Finishing:** Place WS of both pieces tog and sew all around with a backstitch (see page 12), leaving about 3" opening if stuffing pillow or 8" opening if using pillow form. Fold batting to size of pillow and insert into pillow, or insert pillow form. Sew opening closed.

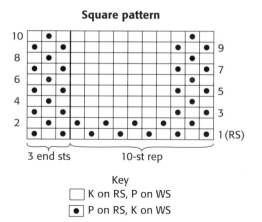

Square pattern

3 end sts   10-st rep

Key

☐ K on RS, P on WS

▣ P on RS, K on WS

Square Pattern

Multiple of 10 + 3

Row 1 (RS): *P1, K1, rep from * to last 3 sts, P1, K1, P1.

Row 2: P1, K1, P1, *K1, P1, rep from * to end.

Row 3: *P1, K1, P1, K7, rep from * to last 3 sts, P1, K1, P1.

Row 4: P1, K1, P1, *P8, K1, P1, rep from * to end.

Rows 5–10: Work rows 3 and 4 another 3 times.

Rep rows 1–10 for patt.

Pillow C

Diamond Pattern

Multiple of 10 + 9

Row 1 (RS): K4, *P1, K9, rep from * to last 5 sts, P1, K4.

Row 2: P3, K1, P1, *K1, P7, K1, P1, rep from * to last 4 sts, K1, P3.

Row 3: K2, P1, K1, *P1, K1, P1, K5, P1, K1, rep from * to last 5 sts, P1, K1, P1, K2.

Row 4: (P1, K1) twice, P1, *K1, P1, K1, P3, (K1, P1) twice, rep from * to last 4 sts, (K1, P1) twice.

Row 5: (P1, K1) twice, *(P1, K1) 5 times, rep from * to last 5 sts, (P1, K1) twice, P1.

Row 6: Rep row 4.

Row 7: Rep row 3.

Row 8: Rep row 2.

Row 9: Rep row 1.

Row 10: Purl.

Rep rows 1–10 for patt.

Pillow

- **Front and back (make 2):** CO 69 sts and work patt 8 times (total 80 rows). BO all sts.

- **Finishing:** Place WS of both pieces tog and sew all around with a backstitch (see page 12), leaving about 3" opening if stuffing pillow or 8" opening if using pillow form. Fold batting to size of pillow and insert into pillow, or insert pillow form. Sew opening closed.

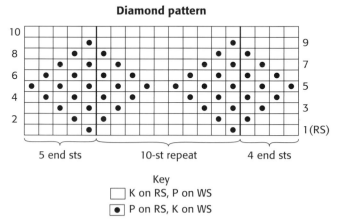

Diamond pattern

5 end sts | 10-st repeat | 4 end sts

Key

☐ K on RS, P on WS

▣ P on RS, K on WS

Baby Bunny

This bunny will be extra special when you knit it for your baby to love, cuddle, and drag around the house. It's washable and the eyes are stitched on—it'll last forever!

Skill Level

■■■□ Intermediate

Finished Length

With ears up: 27"

> *Most of us would do more for our babies than we have ever been willing to do for anyone, even ourselves.*
>
> —Polly Berrien Berends

Materials

- 2 skeins of 220 Superwash from Cascade Yarns (100% superwash wool; 100 g/3.5 oz; 220 yds), in color 839 Pink
- Size 8 needles
- Size 8 double-pointed needles
- Darning needle
- Small bits of yarn in contrasting color for face
- Stuffing

Gauge

18 sts and 24 rows = 4" in St st

Face

- CO 49 sts. Work 12 rows in St st, ending with WS row.

  Row 1 (RS): K5, K2tog, rep from * to end—42 sts.

  Row 2 and all WS rows: Purl.

  Row 3: *K4, K2tog, rep from * to end—35 sts.

  Row 5: *K3, K2tog, rep from * to end—28 sts.

  Row 7: *K2, K2tog, rep from * to end—21 sts.

  Row 9: *K1, K2tog, rep from * to end—14 sts.

  Row 11: K2tog to end—7 sts.

  Row 12: Purl.

- Cut a 12" tail and thread darning needle. Pull tail through rem 7 sts and pull tight. Bring sides tog to form cone shape and use thread tail to sew sides of cone tog, fasten off, and weave in ends.

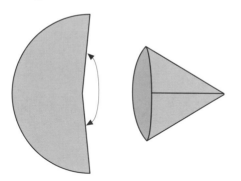

- With darning needle and contrasting yarn, stitch eyes and nose in satin stitch. Stitch mouth as shown above right.

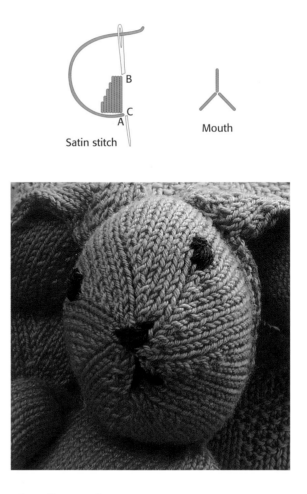

Satin stitch

Mouth

Back of Head

- CO 16 sts (this is top of head). Working in St st, inc in middle of each knit row as follows:

  Row 1: K8, K1f&b, K7—17 sts.

  Row 2 and all WS rows: Purl.

  Row 3: K8, K1f&b, K8—18 sts.

  Row 5: K9, K1f&b, K8—19 sts.

  Row 7: K9, K1f&b, K9—20 sts.

Row 9: K10, K1f&b, K9—21 sts.

Row 11: K10, K1f&b, K10—22 sts.

Row 13: K11, K1f&b, K10—23 sts.

Row 15: K11, K1f&b, K11—24sts.

- Dec 1 st in middle of each knit row as follows:

Row 17: K11, K2tog, K11—23 sts.

Row 19: K10, K2tog, K11—22 sts.

Row 21: K10, K2tog, K10—21 sts.

Row 23: K9, K2tog, K10—20 sts.

- BO 1 st at beg of every row until there are 9 sts. BO all sts.

Ears (Make 4)

- CO 6 sts. Working in St st, inc 1 st in middle of each knit row until there are 18 sts.

Row 1 (RS): K3, K1f&b, K2—7 sts.

Row 2 and all WS rows: Purl.

Row 3: K3, K1f&b, K3—8 sts.

Row 5: K4, K1f&b, K3—9 sts.

Row 7: K4, K1f&b, K4—10 sts.

Row 9: K5, K1f&b, K4—11 sts.

Row 11: K5, K1f&b, K5—12 sts.

Row 13: K6, K1f&b, K5—13 sts.

Row 15: K6, K1f&b, K6—14 sts.

Row 17: K7, K1f&b, K6—15 sts.

Row 19: K7, K1f&b, K7—16 sts.

Row 21: K8, K1f&b, K7—17 sts.

Row 23: K8, K1f&b, K8—18 sts.

- Dec 1 st in middle of each knit row until there are 8 sts.

Row 25: K8, K2tog, K8—17 sts.

Row 27: K8, K2tog, K7—16 sts.

Row 29: K7, K2tog, K7—15 sts.

Row 31: K7, K2tog, K6—14 sts.

Row 33: K6, K2tog, K6—13 sts.

Row 35: K6, K2tog, K5—12 sts.

Row 37: K5, K2tog, K5—11 sts.

Row 39: K5, K2tog, K4—10 sts.

Row 41: K4, K2tog, K4—9 sts.

Row 43: K4, K2tog, K3—8 sts.

- *K2tog to end. Purl 1 row. Rep from * 2 more times. Pull yarn through and fasten off.

Chest

- CO 20 sts. Working in St st, inc 1 st at each side of next 8 rows—36 sts.

- Work in St st until chest measures 6¼".

- Dec 1 st at each side every RS row 5 times—26 sts. Chest should measure approx 8".

Back

- Work same as chest until back measures 6¼".

- Work shaping as follows: K23, ssk, K1, turn. Sl 1, P11, P2tog, P1, turn.

  Row 1: Sl 1 wyib, knit to gap, ssk (one from each side of gap), K1.

Row 2: Sl 1 wyif, purl to gap, P2tog, P1.

Rep rows 1 and 2 until you have worked all sts. Work should measure approx 8". BO all sts.

Arms (Make 2)

- CO 20 sts. Work in St st for 8" and BO all sts.

Legs (Make 2)

- Using dpn, CO 24 sts and divide evenly over 3 needles (8 sts per needle). Join into rnd, pm, and work until leg measures 10".

- **Heel flap:** K6, turn, and P12.

  Row 1: Sl 1 pw wyib, knit to end.

  Row 2: Sl 1 pw wyif, purl to end.

  Rep rows 1 and 2 until 12 rows have been worked and there are 6 selvage sts on each side.

- **Turn heel:** K7, ssk, K1, turn. Sl 1, P4, P2tog, P1, turn.

  Row 1: Sl 1 wyib, knit to gap, ssk (one from each side of gap), K1, turn.

  Row 2: Sl 1 wyif, purl to gap, P2tog, P1, turn.

  Rep rows 1 and 2 until you have worked all sts.

- **Gusset:** Knit across heel sts and PU 6 selvage sts. Knit across instep sts. With new needle PU 6 selvage sts.

- **Side to toe:** *On needle 1, knit to last 3 sts, K2tog, K1. On needle 2, K1, ssk, knit to last 3 sts, K2tog, K1. On needle 3, K1, ssk, knit to end. Rep from * until there are 8 sts.

- Graft toe with kitchener stitch (see page 12).

Finishing

Weave in ends and sew pieces with RS tog as follows:

- Sew face to back of head, leaving small opening. Turn RS out.

- Sew ears tog, then insert open end about 1" into inside of ear. Sew ears to top of head. Stuff head, and sew up opening.

- Stuff legs.

- Sew up arms, leaving small opening. Stuff arms and sew up opening.

- Position legs and arms against RS of back as shown and tack them down using basting stitch. Place chest over top (legs will be sticking out of neck) and pin. Sew chest to back, making sure that legs and arms are firmly in place, and leave opening for turning. Turn RS out and stuff body. Position head on top of body and sew head to body.

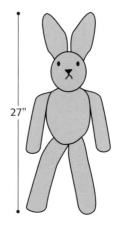

27"

Baby Bunny

Chilly Baby: Hooded Cardigan

For those cold days when your baby needs something warm, this is the perfect sweater.
The wool is soft and breathable and won't make your baby too hot.

Skill Level

■■□□ Easy

Size

9 (12, 18, 24) months

Finished Measurements

Chest: 18¼ (20, 22¾, 25¼)"
Length: 10 (10½, 11, 11½)"

Materials

- Supermerino 101 from Artyarns (100% merino wool; 104 yds) in the following amounts and colors: **4**

  MC   1 skein • color 118 Green
  CC1   1 skein • color 116 Orange
  CC2   1 skein • color 103 Variegated Yellow
- Size 6 needles
- Size 7 needles or size required to obtain gauge
- 4 buttons, ½" diameter

Some men get so excited when they are involved in the birth of their kids that the day-to-day business of child rearing seems an anticlimax by comparison. I asked many men if they could identify their proudest moment as father, and the majority of them said it was the moment the child was born—all the things they had done with the kids and all the children's new accomplishments paled beside this great event.

—S. Adams Sullivan

Gauge

20 sts and 28 rows = 4" in St st on larger needles

Stripe Sequence (Worked in St st)

Work 4 rows with CC2.

Work 4 rows with CC1.

Work 4 rows with CC2.

Work 4 rows with MC.

Rep these 16 rows for stripe sequence.

Back

When changing colors, carry yarns loosely up the side.

- With smaller needles and MC, CO 48 (52, 56, 58) sts. Work K2, P2 ribbing for 4 rows as follows: **All rows:** *K2, P2, rep from * to end of row.

- Switch to larger needles and MC, work 2 rows in St st.

- Change to CC2 and work stripe sequence until back measures 5¼ (5½, 5¾, 6)" from beg, ending with WS row.

- **Armholes:** BO 3 sts at beg of next 2 rows. Work dec row on RS rows 6 times as follows: K1, K2tog, work to last 3 sts, ssk, K1—30 (34, 38, 42) sts. Cont in St st until back measures 3¾ (4, 4¼, 4½)" from beg of armhole, ending with WS row.

- **Beg neck shaping:** K12 (13, 14, 15), BO 6 (8, 10, 12) sts, finish row.

- **Left neck:** Purl 1 row. BO 2 sts at neck, knit to end. Purl 1 row. K2tog at neck, knit to end—9 (10, 11, 12) sts. Purl 1 row. BO rem sts.

- **Right neck:** With WS facing you, attach yarn at neck, BO 2 sts, purl to end. Knit 1 row. P2tog at neck, purl to end—9 (10, 11, 12) sts. Knit 1 row. Purl 1 row. BO rem sts.

Right Front

- With smaller needles and MC, CO 20 (24, 28, 32) sts. Work as for back until armholes.

- **Armhole:** BO 2 (2, 3, 3) sts at beg of next row. P2tog at side on EOR 4 (6, 6, 7) times—14 (16, 19, 22) sts. Cont in St st until piece measures 2¾ (3, 3¼, 3½)" from beg of armhole, ending with WS row.

- **Neck shaping:** BO 2 (2, 3, 3) sts at neck, knit to end. Purl 1 row. *K2tog at neck, knit to end. Purl 1 row. Rep from * 2 (3, 4, 6) times—9 (10, 11, 12) sts. Cont until piece measures same length as back. BO rem sts.

Left Front

- With smaller needles and MC, CO 20 (24, 28, 32) sts. Work as for back until armholes.

- **Armhole:** BO 2 (2, 3, 3) sts at beg of next row. K2tog at side on EOR 4 (6, 6, 7) times—14 (16, 19, 22) sts. Cont in St st until piece measures same as right front, ending with RS row.

- **Neck shaping:** BO 2 (2, 3, 3) sts at neck, purl to end. Knit 1 row. *P2tog at neck, purl to end. Knit 1 row. Rep from * 2 (3, 4, 6) times—9 (10, 11, 12) sts. Cont until piece measures same length as back. BO rem sts.

Sleeves (Make 2)

- With smaller needles and MC, CO 36 (40, 44, 48) sts. Work K2, P2 ribbing for 1½" as follows: **All rows:** *K2, P2, rep from * to end of row.
- Switch to larger needles and CC2. Working in stripe sequence, inc 1 st at each side of every 8 rows 4 times—44 (48, 52, 56) sts. Cont until sleeve measures 6 (6¼, 6½, 6¾)", ending with WS row.
- **Cap shaping:** BO 3 sts at beg of next 2 rows. BO 4 sts at beg of next 7 (8, 9, 10) rows. BO rem 10 sts.

Hood

- Sew shoulder seams.
- With larger needles and RS facing you, starting at right front edge, PU 12 (13, 14, 15) sts to shoulder, 24 (26, 28, 30) sts across back neck, 12 (13, 14, 15) sts from shoulder to left front. Purl 1 row. Work in St st until hood measures 6¾ (7, 7¼, 7½)" from PU.

Finishing

- **Neck and front bands.** With RS facing you, beg at bottom front edge, PU 170 (174, 178, 182) sts around to opposite front edge. Work K2, P2 ribbing for 1 row. Work next row (buttonhole row on right-hand side for girls and on left-hand side for boys) as follows: Maintaining ribbing patt, make 4 buttonholes evenly spaced by working YO, K2tog for each buttonhole. Work 2 more rows in ribbing. BO all sts.
- Sew in sleeves. Sew side seams.
- Sew on buttons.
- Block sweater.

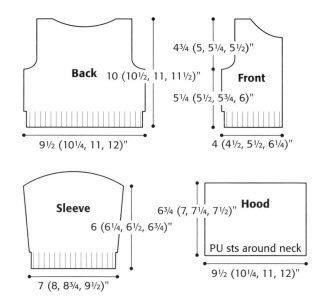

Pretty Baby: Coatdress and Hat

When a special occasion arises, everyone wants to look his or her best. This coatdress will be an ideal fit anywhere your little girl goes. The hat adds that picture-perfect touch that's just right.

Skill Level

■■■□ Intermediate

Size

One size (fits 12 to 18 months)

Finished Measurements

Chest: 24"

Length: 20½"

Hat circumference: 16"

Materials

- 2 hanks of Laurel from the Schaefer Yarn Company (100% mercerized pima cotton; 8 oz; 400 yds) in color Emily Dickinson ④
- Size 10 straight needles, 16" circular needle, and double-pointed needles or size required to obtain gauge
- Size 8 needles for neck and front bands

Gauge

18 sts and 24 rows = 4" in St st on larger needles

Somehow I managed to get through those years with all those babies. I don't know how I did it. When you're young, you think everything is exciting. When you get older you say, "How in the world did I do that?"

—Loretta Lynn

Coatdress

Back

MB: (K1, P1, K1, P1) in next st (4 sts), turn, P4, turn, K4, turn, P2tog twice, turn and K2tog.

- With larger straight needles, CO 89 sts and work bottom border as follows:

  Row 1 (WS): Knit.

  Row 2: K2, *MB, K5, rep from * to last 3 sts, MB, K2.

  Row 3: Knit.

  Row 4: K2tog, knit to last 2 sts, K2tog.

- Beg St st, dec 1 st at each side every 5 rows 15 times—57 sts. Work should measure approx 15", ending with WS row.

- **Armholes:** BO 4 sts at beg of next 2 rows. BO 2 sts at beg of next 2 rows. Dec 1 st at each side on next row—43 sts. Cont in St st until piece measures 4½" from beg of armhole, ending with WS row.

- **Beg neck shaping:** K17, BO 9 sts, finish row.

- **Left neck:** Purl 1 row. BO 2 sts at neck, knit to end. *Purl to last 2 sts, P2tog. K2tog at neck, knit to end. Rep from * once. Purl to last 2 sts, P2tog—10 sts. BO all sts.

- **Right neck:** With WS facing you, attach yarn at neck edge, BO 2 sts, purl to end. *Knit to last 2 sts, K2tog. P2tog at neck, purl to end. Rep from * once. Knit to last 2 sts, K2tog—10 sts. BO all sts.

Left Front

- With larger straight needles, CO 47 sts and work bottom border as follows:

  Row 1 (WS): Knit.

  Row 2: K2, *MB, K5, rep from * to last 3 sts, MB, K2.

  Row 3: Knit.

  Row 4: K2tog, knit to end—46 sts.

- Beg St st on WS row and work as follows:

  WS row: Sl first st kw tbl, K1, purl to end.

  RS row: Knit.

  Rep last 2 rows, dec 1 st at side every 5 rows 17 times—29 sts. Note that decs will alternate at beg or end of every fifth row depending on whether it is purl or knit row.

- AT SAME TIME when work measures 4½", and on row 26 (RS), work button row as follows: Knit to last 3 sts, MB, K2. This creates button at center front. Rep button row every 18 rows 2 more times, then every 10 rows 4 more times.

- **Armhole shaping:** When work measures 15" from beg, with RS facing, BO 4 sts at beg of next row. BO 2 sts at beg of next RS row. BO 1 st at beg of next RS row—22 sts. Cont in St st until piece measures 3½" from beg of armhole and last button has been made. Work 2 rows, ending with RS row.

- **Neck shaping:** BO 5 sts at neck, purl to end. Knit 1 row. BO 3 sts at neck, purl to end. Knit 1 row. BO 1 st at neck on next 4 RS rows—10 sts. BO all sts.

Right Front

- Work buttonhole as follows:

  Row 1: Work to placement of buttonhole, YO twice, K2tog tbl.

  Row 2: Work to YOs, purl first YO and drop 2nd YO from needle.

- With larger straight needles, CO 47 sts and work bottom border as follows:

  Row 1 (WS): Knit.

  Row 2: K2, *MB, K5, rep from * to last 3 sts, MB, K2.

  Row 3: Knit.

  Row 4: Knit to last 2 sts, K2tog—46 sts.

- Beg St st on WS row and work as follows:

  WS rows: Purl to last st, K1.

  RS rows: P1, knit to end.

  Rep last 2 rows, dec 1 st at side every 5 rows 17 times—29 sts. Note that decs will alternate at beg or end of every fifth row depending on whether it is purl or knit row.

- AT SAME TIME when piece measures 4½", and on row 26 (RS), work buttonhole row as follows: P1, K3, work buttonhole as above, knit to end. Rep buttonhole row every 18 rows 2 more times, and then every 10 rows 4 times.

- **Armhole shaping:** When work measures 15" from beg, ending with WS row, BO 4 sts at beg of next row. BO 2 sts at beg of next WS row. BO 1 st at

beg of next WS row—22 sts. Cont in St st until piece measures 3½" from beg of armhole and last buttonhole has been worked, ending with WS row.

- **Neck shaping:** BO 5 sts at neck, knit to end. Purl 1 row. BO 3 sts at neck, knit to end. Purl 1 row. BO 1 st at neck on next 4 RS rows—10 sts. BO all sts.

Sleeves (Make 2)

- With larger straight needles, CO 35 sts and work bottom border as follows:

  Row 1 (WS): Knit.

  Row 2: K2, *MB, K5, rep from * to last 3 sts, MB, K2.

  Rows 3 and 4: Knit.

- Beg St st with WS row, then inc 1 st at each side every 12 rows 5 times—45 sts. Work even until sleeve measures 8¾", ending with WS row.

- **Cap shaping:** BO 4 sts at beg of next 2 rows. BO 2 sts at beg of next 4 rows. BO 3 sts at beg of next 5 rows. BO 4 sts at beg of next 2 rows. BO rem 6 sts.

Finishing

- Weave in ends.

- Sew shoulder seams.

- Sew in sleeves. Sew side seams.

- **Front edge on buttonhole side:** With smaller needles, PU 82 sts along front with buttonholes. Knit 2 rows and BO all sts.

- **Neckband:** With smaller needles, beg at right front, PU 18 sts to shoulder, 26 sts across back neck, 18 sts from shoulder to left front—62 sts. Knit 2 rows and BO all sts.

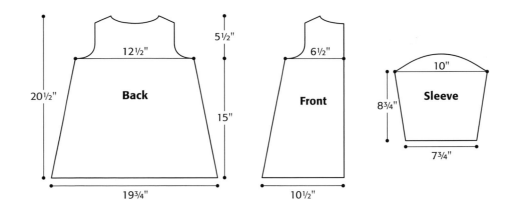

Hat

Switch to dpns when necessary.

- With circular needle, CO 71 sts and work bottom border back and forth as follows:

  Row 1 (WS): Knit.

  Row 2: K2, *MB, K5, rep from * to last 3 sts, MB, K2.

  Rows 3 and 4: Knit.

- With RS facing you, join into rnd and knit 1 rnd. When you reach end of rnd, K2tog (1 st from beg and 1 from end), pm—70 sts.

- Knit until hat measures 3" from beg. Purl 2 rnds.

- Work dec as follows:

  *K8, K2tog, rep from * around—63 sts.

  Knit 1 rnd.

  *K7, K2tog, rep from * around—56 sts.

  Knit 1 rnd.

  *K6, K2tog, rep from * around—49 sts.

Knit 1 rnd.

*K5, K2tog, rep from * around—42 sts.

Knit 1 rnd.

*K4, K2tog, rep from * around—35 sts.

*K3, K2tog, rep from * around—28 sts.

*K2, K2tog, rep from * around   21 sts.

*K1, K2tog, rep from * around—14 sts.

K2tog in each rnd until 3 sts rem. P3tog. MB in rem st and fasten off.

- Sew seam at bottom of hat.

- Weave in ends.

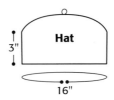

Rock-a-Bye Baby: Reversible Blanket

These soft and snuggly blankets are perfect for those times
when a light blanket is just what the baby ordered.

Skill Level

■■□□ Easy

Size

Small (large)

Finished Measurements

30" x 30 (38)"

Pat-a-cake, pat-a-cake, baker's man,
Bake me a cake as fast as you can;
Pat it and prick it, and mark it with B,
Put it in the oven for baby and me.

Traditional Nursery Rhyme

Materials

- 220 Superwash from Cascade Yarns (100% superwash wool; 100 g/3.5 oz; 220 yds) in the following amounts and colors: **4**

Blue version

Dark	2 skeins	• color 844 Blue
Light	2 skeins	• color 817 Off-White

Pink version

Dark	2 skeins	• color 837 Pink
Light	2 skeins	• color 817 Off-White

- Size 8 circular needle (24") or size required to obtain gauge

Gauge

18 sts and 24 rows = 4"

Read This Before Starting!

Reversible knitting creates a design that is the same on both sides. To begin, cast on with the dark yarn, then slide the stitches to the other end of the circular needle. Join the light yarn and begin the reversible pattern with row 1. Do not cut the yarns at the ends of the rows, but carry them up the side.

- With dark yarn, CO 127 (161) sts. Slide sts to other end of circular needle. Join light yarn and beg reversible patt:

Row 1: With light yarn, K1, *P1, K1, rep from *. Turn.

Row 2: With light yarn, P1, *K1, P1, rep from *. Slide.

Rows 3 and 4: With dark yarn, rep rows 1 and 2.

Rep rows 1–4 until blanket is desired length.

- Weave in ends.
- Block blanket.

One for My Baby: Felted Diaper Bag

This diaper bag was made with mothers in mind. The large pockets will hold everything from bottles to toys to a pacifier, leaving room for larger items inside the bag. There's no rummaging through your bag to find things, so you have more time to play with your baby.

Skill Level

◼◼◼◻ Intermediate

Size

One size (approximate finished measurements after felting: 12" wide x 10½" high x 5½" deep)

> *When the first baby laughed for the first time, the laugh broke into a thousand pieces and they all went skipping about, and that was the beginning of fairies.*
>
> —J. M. Barrie

Materials

- Hand-dyed wool yarn from Rio de la Plata Yarns (100% pure new wool; 3.5 oz; 140 yds) in the following amounts and colors: ④

    MC   7 skeins • color M-59 Multicolor (Yellow, Acid Green, and Blue Violet)

    CC   1 skein • color A-23 Blue Violet

- Size 11 circular needle (29") and double-pointed needles or size required to obtain gauge

- Stitch marker

Gauge

14 sts and 22 rows = 4" in St st

Note: Use 1 strand of yarn for pockets and bag and 2 strands of yarn for straps.

Pockets

- **First side pocket:** With MC and circular needle, CO 65 sts. Work in garter st for 12".

- **End pockets and bag bottom:** Cable CO 35 sts, knit to end. Turn and cable CO 35 sts. Work in garter st for 9".

- **Second side pocket:** On next row, BO 35 sts, work to end. Turn and BO 35 sts. Work rem 65 sts in garter st for 12". BO all sts.

Body of Bag

- Referring to diagram at right, and with MC, PU 65 sts along side A, 25 sts along side B, 65 sts along side C and 25 sts along side D—180 sts. Join into rnd and pm. Knit every rnd for 17".

- Change to CC and work 5 rnds.

- **Eyelet rnd:** K9, BO 3 sts, K39, BO 3 sts, K14, BO 3 sts, K7, BO 3 sts, K14, BO 3 sts, K39, BO 3 sts, K14, BO 3 sts, K7, BO 3 sts, K5.

- Knit next rnd, CO 3 sts over each set of BO sts.

- Knit 5 rnds. Purl 3 rnds. BO all sts.

- Fold bound-off edge toward inside of bag to where you began to purl; sew edge to bag.

- **Straps:** With double-pointed needles and 2 strands of yarn held tog, CO 3 sts and work I-cord for 70" (see page 12).

- Weave cord through holes as shown and sew ends tog.

Finishing

- Sew pockets to sides of bag along all 4 corners and also down middle of large side pockets.

- **Felt bag:** Place bag in zippered bag or pillow protector. Set washer for hot wash, low water level, and maximum agitation. Add small amount of detergent. Check felting about midway. When cycle is finished, remove diaper bag from zippered bag and smooth fabric of diaper bag (sometimes it looks wrinkled), smoothing as you go to ensure correct shape. When bag is in shape you want, place bag upside down over something about the same shape and size that will allow bag to dry.

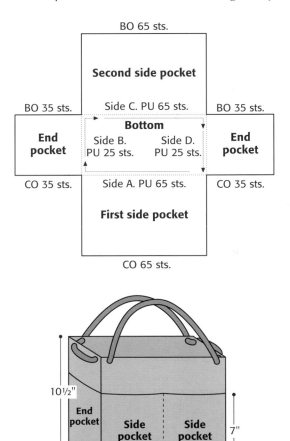

Baby, It's Cold Outside: Boy's Outfit

My friend Jane created this outfit. We were talking one day and playing with our yarn, and this beautiful suit is the end of that story. Put a pair of boots on your little one and it's snowman time!

Skill Level

◧■◻◻ Easy

Size

One size (fits 12 to 18 months)

Finished Measurements

Chest: 25"

Jacket length: 13"

Pants length: 15½"

Hat circumference: 17¾"

Materials

- **A** 1 skein of Bulky Leisure from Cascade Yarns (50% superfine alpaca, 50% pima cotton; 100 g/3.5 oz; 127 yds) in color 8010 Ecru **⑤**
- **B** 4 skeins of 220 Superwash from Cascade Yarns (100% superwash wool; 100 g/3.5 oz; 220 yds) in color 844 Blue **④**
- Size 7 needles
- Size 8 needles or size required to obtain gauge
- Size 10 needles
- ½"-wide elastic, enough to go around waist plus 2"
- 4 buttons, 1" diameter

Gauge

18 sts and 24 rows = 4" in St st with medium needles and B

Seed Stitch

All rows: K1, *P1, K1, rep from * to end.

Pants

One Half (Make 2)

- With larger needles and A, CO 32 sts. Beg with purl row, work 8 rows in St st. Change to medium needles and B. Knit next row on WS, inc 19 sts evenly across row—51 sts. This is fold line for hem. Work 12 rows in St st beg with purl row.

- Cont in St st, inc 1 st at each end of next row and then every fourth row 10 times—73 sts. Work even until piece measures 10" from beg, ending with WS row. Knit 1 row. Purl 1 row. BO 5 sts at beg of next 2 rows. Dec 1 st at each edge on next 3 RS rows—57 sts.

- Work even until piece measures 16" from beg, ending with RS row. Knit 1 row on WS (this is fold line for casing). Work 4 more rows in St st. BO all sts.

- **Finishing:** With RS tog, sew front and back seams from waist to crotch. Sew inside leg seams, reversing seams at cuff so that seam is on correct side after folding cuff up. Fold casing at fold line and sew in place, leaving opening for elastic. Insert elastic into casing, sew ends of elastic tog, and finish seam. Tack bottom cuff to pant leg to keep in place.

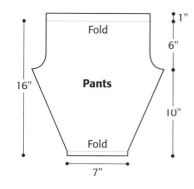

Jacket

Back

- With smaller needles and B, CO 61 sts. Work 8 rows in seed st. Change to medium needles and work in St st until piece measures 8" from beg, ending with WS row.

- **Armholes:** BO 3 sts at beg of next 2 rows. Dec 1 st at each edge every RS row 5 times—45 sts. Work even for 3", ending with WS row.

- **Beg neck shaping:** K15, BO 15 sts, finish row.

- **Left neck:** Dec 1 st at neck edge on next 2 RS rows—13 sts. BO at sts.

- **Right neck:** Attach yarn on WS at neck, dec 1 st at neck. Dec 1 st at neck on next WS row—13 sts. BO all sts.

Left Front

- With smaller needles and B, CO 27 sts. Work 8 rows in seed st. Change to medium needles and work in St st until piece measures 8" from beg, ending with WS row.

- **Armholes:** BO 3 sts at beg of next row. Dec 1 st at side every RS row 5 times—19 sts. Work even until side measures 2½" from beg of armhole, ending with RS row.

- **Neck shaping:** BO 3 sts at neck. Dec 1 st at neck every WS row 3 times—13 sts. BO all sts.

Right Front

- Work as for left front until piece measures 8" from beg, ending with RS row.

- **Armholes:** BO 3 sts at beg of next row. Dec 1 st at side every WS row 5 times—19 sts. Work even until side measures 2½" from beg of armhole, ending with WS row.

- **Neck shaping:** BO 3 sts at neck. Dec 1 st at neck every RS row 3 times—13 sts. BO all sts.

Sleeves (Make 2)

- With larger needles and A, CO 27 sts. Beg with purl row, work 8 rows in St st. Change to medium needles and B. On next row inc 12 sts evenly across row—39 sts. Work even for 2", ending with WS row. Inc 1 st at each edge on next row and every 4 rows 7 times—55 sts. Work even until sleeve measures 8" from beg, ending with WS row.

- **Cap shaping:** BO 3 sts at beg of next 2 rows. Dec 1 st at each edge every RS row 5 times—39 sts. Work even for 3 rows. BO 5 sts at beg of next 6 rows—9 sts. BO all sts.

Front Bands

- **Button band:** With smaller needles and A, CO 7 sts. Work 8 rows in seed st; then change to medium needles and work 66 rows or 11" in seed st. BO all sts. Mark for placement of buttons.

- **Buttonhole band:** Work same as button band, working YO, K2tog to correspond with button placement on button band.

Finishing

- Block all pieces. Sew shoulder seams. Sew bands to front of jacket—buttonhole band on right front for girls and on left front for boys.

- **Collar:** With RS facing you and with smaller needles and B, beg in center of right front band, PU 16 sts from shoulder, 24 sts across back neck, 16 sts from shoulder to left front—56 sts. Change to larger needles and A, K2tog across—28 sts. Beg with knit row, work in St st, inc 1 st at each edge on third row once, and then EOR 5 times—38 sts. BO all sts on RS row.

- Sew on buttons.

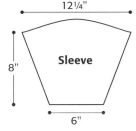

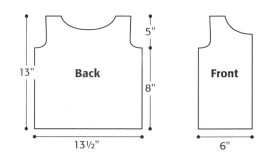

The best way to make children good is to make them happy.
—Oscar Wilde

Hat

- With larger needles and A, CO 40 sts. Beg with purl row, work 12 rows in St st. Change to medium needles and B. Knit 1 row on WS; this is fold line for brim. On next row, K1f&b in each st—80 sts. Beg with purl row, work 3" in St st, ending with WS row.

- Work decs as follows:

  Row 1 (RS): *K6, K2tog, rep from * to end—70 sts.

  Row 2 and all WS rows: Purl.

  Row 3: *K5, K2tog, rep from * to end—60 sts.

  Row 5: *K4, K2tog, rep from * to end—50 sts.

  Row 7: *K3, K2tog, rep from * to end—40 sts.

  Row 9: *K2, K2tog, rep from * to end—30 sts.

  Row 11: *K1, K2tog, rep from * to end—20 sts.

  Row 13: K2tog across—10 sts.

  Row 14: P2tog across—5 sts.

  Row 15: K2tog twice, K1—3 sts.

- Work I-cord (see page 12) on rem 3 sts for 1". BO and sew tail to top of hat. Weave in end.

- Sew seam, reversing seam along brim so that when folded up, seam doesn't show.

- Block garments and hat.

3"

Hat

17¾"

Baby Booties and Mommy Socks

I always loved wearing something to match my babies' outfits. I'm not sure they liked it, but they really didn't have a say, until recently. So while you're still in control of clothing, take charge and wear something to match your baby—it's fun!

Skill Level

■■■□ Intermediate

Sizes

Baby and adult

Finished Length from Heel to Toe

Baby booties: 3½", 4", or 4½" (depending on needle size used)

Adult socks: 8½" (to fit women's shoe size 6 to 9)

Materials

- 1 skein of 220 Superwash from Cascade Yarns (100% Superwash wool; 100 g/3.5 oz; 220 yds). The following colors were used for the models: color 837 Pink, color 843 Purple, color 850 Green, and color 826 Peach. **④**

Note: One skein will yield 3 pairs of baby booties or 1 pair of baby booties and 1 pair of adult socks.

- **Needles for adult socks:**

  Size 6 double-pointed needles

  Size 7 double-pointed needles

- **Needles for baby booties:**

  - 3½" length

  Size 5 double-pointed needles

  Size 6 double-pointed needles

  - 4" length

  Size 6 double-pointed needles

  Size 7 double-pointed needles

  - 4½" length

  Size 7 double-pointed needles

  Size 8 double-pointed needles

- Stitch holder
- Tapestry needle

Gauge

22 sts and 24 rows = 4" in St st on size 6 needles

20 sts and 22 rows = 4" in St st on size 7 needles

18 sts and 20 rows = 4" in St st on size 8 needles

People often ask us, "How do you do it?" Or they say, "I could never deal with seven babies at one time." My confidence lies in knowing that God promises never to ask us to do anything He doesn't enable and equip us for. He blessed us with our children. We can have every confidence that He will provide the strength, the wisdom, and the resources we need to raise them.

—Bobbi McCaughey

Adult Socks (Make 2)

- With larger needles, CO 44 sts and divide sts evenly onto 4 needles (11 sts each). Knit 1 rnd. Switch to smaller needles and knit 5 rnds. Switch to larger needles and knit 1 rnd.

- **Heel flap:** K11, turn, and P22. Place rem 22 sts on holder for instep. Work heel flap on 22 sts as follows:

  Row 1: Sl 1 wyib, knit across.

  Row 2: Sl 1 wyif, purl across.

  Rep rows 1 and 2 for total of 22 rows.

- **Turn heel:**

  Row 1: K13, ssk, K1, turn.

  Row 2: Sl 1 wyif, P5, P2tog, P1, turn.

  Row 3: Sl 1 wyib, knit to 1 st before gap, ssk (1 st from each side of gap), K1, turn.

  Row 4: Sl 1 wyif, purl to 1 st before gap, P2tog, P1, turn.

  Rep rows 3 and 4 until all heel sts have been worked, ending with WS row—14 sts.

- **Heel gusset:** Sts will be divided on 3 needles from this point. Knit across heel sts and PU 11 selvage sts on same needle. With another needle, knit across instep. With new needle, PU 11 selvage sts, then knit 7 heel sts. You should have 18 sts each on needles 1 and 3, and 22 sts on needle 2—58 sts total.

  Rnd 1: On needle 1, knit to last 3 sts, K2tog, K1. On needle 2, knit across instep. On needle 3, K1, ssk, knit to end.

  Rnd 2: Knit.

  Rep rnds 1 and 2 until 11 sts rem on needles 1 and 3. Knit for 2½" from decs (longer or shorter depending on foot size) or 6½" from heel. (These socks were made for women with size 8 feet— adjust accordingly.)

- **Toe dec:**

  Rnd 1: On needle 1, knit to last 3 sts, K2tog, K1. On needle 2, K1, ssk, work to last 3 sts, K2tog, K1. On needle 3, K1, ssk, knit to end.

  Rnd 2: Knit.

  Rep rnds 1 and 2 until total of 20 sts rem.

  Rep rnd 1 until total of 8 sts rem. Knit 2 sts on needle 1 once more, then move them to needle 3. This will give you 4 instep sts on one needle and 4 sts from bottom part of sock on other needle. Cut yarn, leaving 12" tail to graft toe.

- Graft toe with kitchener stitch (see page 12).

- Weave in ends.

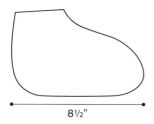

8½"

Baby Booties and Mommy Socks

Baby Socks (Make 2)

- With larger needles, CO 28 sts and divide evenly onto 4 needles (7 sts on each needle). Knit 1 rnd. Switch to smaller needles and knit 5 rnds. Switch to larger needles and knit 1 rnd.

- **Heel flap:** K7, turn, and P14. Place rem 14 sts on holder for instep. Work heel flap on 14 sts as follows:

  Row 1: Sl 1 wyib, knit across.

  Row 2: Sl 1 wyif, purl across.

  Rep rows 1 and 2 for total of 14 rows.

- **Turn heel:**

  Row 1: K9, ssk, K1, turn.

  Row 2: Sl 1 wyif, P5, P2tog, P1, turn.

  Row 3: Sl 1 wyib, knit to 1 st before gap, ssk (1 st from each side of gap), K1, turn.

  Row 4: Sl 1 wyif, purl to 1 st before gap, P2tog, P1, turn—10 sts.

- **Heel gusset:** Sts will be divided on 3 needles from this point. Knit across heel sts and PU 7 selvage sts on same needle. With another needle, knit across instep. With new needle, PU 7 selvage sts, then knit 5 heel sts. You should have 12 sts each on needles 1 and 3, and 14 sts on needle 2—38 sts total.

  Rnd 1: On needle 1, knit to last 3 sts, K2tog, K1. On needle 2, knit across instep. On needle 3, K1, ssk, knit to end.

  Rnd 2: Knit.

  Rep rnds 1 and 2 until 7 sts rem on needles 1 and 3. Knit 4 rnds (work more or fewer rnds depending on foot size).

- **Toe dec rnd:** On needle 1, knit to last 3 sts, K2tog, K1. On needle 2, K1, ssk, work to last 3 sts, K2tog, K1. On needle 3, K1, ssk, knit to end.

- Rep dec rnd until total of 8 sts rem. Work rem decs as follows: On needle 1, K2tog. On needle 2, ssk, K2tog. On needle 3, ssk. Cut yarn leaving 8" tail. Thread tail on tapestry needle and pull through rem 4 sts. Pull tightly to close toe.

- Weave in ends.

3½ (4, 4½)"

Three Hats for Baby

As every mother knows, a baby's head gets cold. Slip one of these cozy caps into your diaper bag and you'll have it handy when your little angel needs a hat.

Skill Level

◣■☐◗ Easy

Finished Circumference

Hat A: 13½ (15¾, 18)"

Hat B: 13¾ (15½, 17)"

Hat C: 13½ (15, 16½)"

Materials

Hat A

- 1 skein of Merino Style from Knit Picks (100% merino wool; 50 g; 123 yds) in color 23452 Tide Pool **(3)**

- Size 5 circular needle (16") and double-pointed needles or size required to obtain gauge. (If you are making the smallest size, you will need only double-pointed needles.)

- Stitch marker

Hat B

- 1 skein of Sock Garden from Knit Picks (100% merino wool; 50 g; 220 yds) in color 23468 Star Gazer Lily **(1)**

- Size 3 circular needle (16") and double-pointed needles or size required to obtain gauge

- Stitch marker

Hat C

- 1 skein of Twirl from Knit Picks (69% superfine alpaca, 28% wool, 3% nylon; 100 g; 67 yds) in color 2588 Summer Sky **(5)**

- Size 9 circular needle (16") and double-pointed needles or size required to obtain gauge

- Stitch marker

Note: If you prefer to work hats with double-pointed needles, you will not need circular needles.

Gauge

Hat A: 18 sts and 32 rows = 4"

Hat B: 28 sts and 36 rows = 4"

Hat C: 16 sts and 18 rows = 4"

Hat A

Switch to dpns when necessary.

- Using circular needle, CO 60 (70, 80) sts. Join into rnd, pm, and work seed st patt as follows:

    Rnd 1: *K1, P1, rep from * around.

    Rnd 2: *P1, K1, rep from * around.

    Rep rnds 1 and 2 for total of 16 rnds.

- Knit 8 rnds.
- Work seed st patt for 8 rnds.
- Knit 4 rnds.
- Work seed st patt for 4 rnds.
- Knit 1 rnd.

- Work dec rnds as follows:

    *K8, K2tog, rep from * around—54 (63, 72) sts. Knit 1 rnd.

    *K7, K2tog, rep from * around—48 (56, 64) sts. Knit 1 rnd.

    *K6, K2tog, rep from * around—42 (49, 56) sts. Knit 1 rnd.

    *K5, K2tog, rep from * around—36 (42, 48) sts. Knit 1 rnd.

    *K4, K2tog, rep from * around—30 (35, 40) sts. Knit 1 rnd.

    *K3, K2tog, rep from * around—24 (28, 32) sts. Knit 1 rnd.

    *K2, K2tog, rep from * around—18 (21, 24) sts. Knit 1 rnd.

    *K1, K2tog, rep from * around—12 (14, 16) sts. Knit 1 rnd.

    *K2tog until 3 sts rem.

- Work I-cord (see page 12) on 3 rem sts for 2". K3tog, pull yarn through last loop, and sew loop to top of hat.
- Weave in ends.

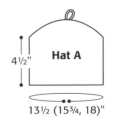

4½"   **Hat A**

13½ (15¾, 18)"

Hat B

Switch to dpns when necessary.

- Using circular needle, CO 96 (108, 120) sts. Join into rnd, pm, and work ribbing as follows:

  All rnds: *K1, P1, rep from * to end.

  Work ribbing until hat measures 1½".

- Knit until hat measures 3¼ (3½, 3¾)".

- Work dec as follows:

  *K10, K2tog, rep from * around—88 (99, 110) sts.

  Knit 3 rnds.

  *K9, K2tog, rep from * around—80 (90, 100) sts.

  Knit 3 rnds.

*K8, K2tog, rep from * around—72 (81, 90) sts.

Knit 2 rnds.

*K7, K2tog, rep from * around—64 (72, 80) sts.

Knit 2 rnds.

*K6, K2tog, rep from * around—56 (63, 70) sts.

Knit 1 rnd.

*K5, K2tog, rep from * around—48 (54, 60) sts.

Knit 1 rnd.

*K4, K2tog, rep from * around—40 (45, 50) sts.

Knit 1 rnd.

*K3, K2tog, rep from * around—32 (36, 40) sts.

Knit 2 rnds.

*K2, K2tog, rep from * around—24 (27, 30) sts.

Knit 2 rnds.

*K1, K2tog, rep from * around—16 (18, 20) sts.

Knit 3 rnds.

K2tog until 3 sts rem. K3tog, pull yarn through last loop, and fasten off.

- Weave in ends.

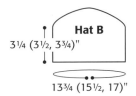

Hat B

3¼ (3½, 3¾)"

13¾ (15½, 17)"

Hat C

Switch to dpns when necessary.

- Using circular needle, CO 60 (66, 72) sts. Join into rnd, pm, and work dec as follows:

  *K8 (9, 10), K2tog, rep from * around—54 (60, 66) sts.

  Knit 1 rnd.

  *K7 (8, 9), K2tog, rep from * around—48 (54, 60 sts.

  Knit 2 rnds.

  *K6 (7, 8), K2tog, rep from * around—42 (48, 54) sts.

- Knit even until hat measures 4" from last dec row.

- Work dec as follows:

  *K5 (6, 7), K2tog, rep from * around—36 (42, 48) sts.

  Knit 1 rnd.

  *K4 (5, 6), K2tog, rep from * around—30 (36, 42) sts.

  Knit 1 rnd.

  *K3 (4, 5), K2tog, rep from * around—24 (30, 36) sts.

  Knit 1 rnd.

  *K2 (3, 4), K2tog, rep from * around—18 (24, 30) sts.

  Knit 1 rnd.

  *K1 (2, 3), K2tog, rep from * around—12 (18, 24) sts.

  Knit 1 rnd.

  *K0 (1, 2), K2tog, rep from * around—6 (12, 18) sts.

  Knit 1 rnd.

  K2tog around until 2 (3, 3) sts rem. K2 (3, 3) tog, pull yarn through last loop, and fasten off.

- Weave in ends.

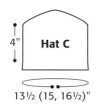

Hat C

4"

13½ (15, 16½)"

Three Hats for Baby

God Bless the Child: Reversible Blanket

When my babies were small, I decorated their rooms with yellow, red, and blue. This blanket reminds me of those days when I first brought my babies home. The yarn I selected for this blanket is some of the softest yarn I've used. Your baby will love snuggling up in it well into his or her teens, if the blanket lasts that long.

Skill Level

■□□□ Beginner

Size

One size

Finished Measurements

36" x 42"

Materials

- 14 skeins of Crayon from Knit Picks (100% pima cotton; 50 g; 128 yds) in color 23608 (3)
- Size 10 needles or size required to obtain gauge

Gauge

11½ sts and 19 rows = 4" in patt st with 2 strands of yarn held tog

> There are only two lasting bequests we can hope to give our children. One of these is roots; the other, wings.
>
> —Hodding Carter

Pattern Stitch

(Multiple of 6 sts + 2)

Row 1: Sl 1 wyib, *K4, P2, rep from * to last st, K1.

Row 2: Sl 1 wyif, *K2, P4, rep from * to last st, K1.

Row 3: Rep row 1.

Row 4: Sl 1 wyif, *P2, K4, rep from * to last st, K1.

Row 5: Sl 1 wyib, *P4, K2, rep from * to last st, K1.

Row 6: Rep row 4.

Rep rows 1–6 for patt.

Blanket

- With 2 strands of yarn held tog, CO 146 sts.
- Work patt st until blanket measures approx 36", ending with completed row 5.
- BO in patt.
- Weave in ends.

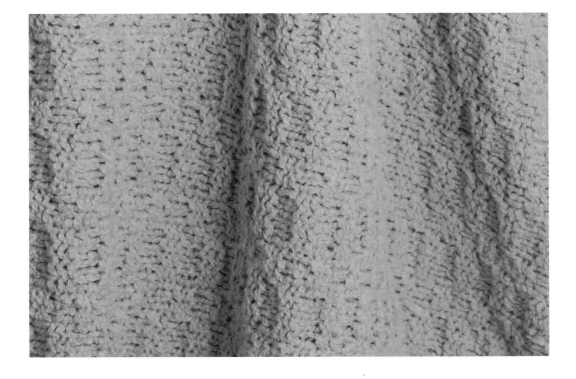

Useful Information

Standard Yarn-Weight System

Yarn-Weight Symbol and Category Names	Super Fine **1**	Fine **2**	Light **3**	Medium **4**	Bulky **5**	Super Bulky **6**
Types of Yarns in Category	Sock, Fingering, Baby	Sport, Baby	DK, Light Worsted	Worsted, Afghan, Aran	Chunky, Craft, Rug	Bulky, Roving
Knit Gauge Ranges in Stockinette Stitch to 4"	27 to 32 sts	23 to 26 sts	21 to 24 sts	16 to 20 sts	12 to 15 sts	6 to 11 sts
Recommended Needle in U.S. Size Range	1 to 3	3 to 5	5 to 7	7 to 9	9 to 11	11 and larger

Metric Conversions

m = yds x 0.9144

yds = m x 1.0936

g = oz x 28.35

oz = g x 0.0352

Skill Levels

Beginner: Projects for first-time knitters using basic knit and purl stitches. Minimal shaping.

Easy: Projects using basic stitches, repetitive stitch patterns, and simple color changes. Simple shaping and finishing.

Intermediate: Projects using a variety of stitches, such as basic cables and lace, simple intarsia, and techniques for double-pointed needles and knitting in the round. Mid-level shaping and finishing.

Resources

Contact the following companies to find shops that carry the yarns and decorative items featured in this book.

Artyarns Inc.

www.artyarns.com

Supermerino 101

Ultramerino 6

Wool Fur

Cascade Yarns

www.cascadeyarns.com

220 Superwash

Bulky Leisure

Pima Tencel

Sierra

Debbie's Clayground

www.debbiesclayground.com

Buttons and pins

Frog Tree

508-385-8862

PO Box 1119

East Dennis, MA 02641

Pima Silk

Knit Picks

www.knitpicks.com

Crayon

Merino Style

Sock Garden

Twirl

Kollage Yarns

www.kollageyarns.com

Passion

Romance

Rio de la Plata Yarns

www.riodelaplatayarns.com

Hand-dyed wool yarn

The Schaefer Yarn Company Ltd.

www.schaeferyarn.com

Laurel

About the Author

*L*ynda Schar learned to knit at age seven while living in South Africa. Since then she has embraced knitting as an essential part of her life. In addition to designing, Lynda teaches knitting to anyone who will sit still long enough to learn. She lives in Keizer, Oregon, with her husband, Kurt, and daughter Vanessa along with their cats, CoCo and Bert. She also has her own business, 1knitwit2purl pattern company. For more of her designs, visit her Web site at www.1knitwit2purl.com.